# YOUR JOURNAL OF
# DEPERSONALISATION DEREALIZATION DISORDER
## MANAGEMENT

Depersonalisation Derealization Disorder has a complex array of causes from Tauma, Stress, and more and can causes an even more complex set of symptoms, from feeling detatched from everything, feeling as if you are observing your thoughts, altered sensations, visual changes and more.

This journal is to help track your symptoms, to find your triggers, write down your thoughts and feelings and to supplement your therapy with worksheets and trigger tracking.

With weekly stress and mood journals, social anxiety symptom and self-care checklists and little worksheets.

**This journal also has gratitude prompts, self-esteem prompts and inspirational quotes to encourage self-care and a positive mindset. To help refocus your mind on your bad days and remind you why life is GREAT!**

This book is also a journal with many lined pages in this journal your thoughts and track achievements on the lined pages.

# DAILY ENERGY vs MOOD TRACKER

TRACK YOUR DAILY ENERGY AND MOOD USING DIFFERENT COLOURS ON THIS LINE CHART - NOTE YOUR TRIGGERS BELOW.

| ENERGY | | MONDAY | TUESDAY | WEDNESDAY | THURSDAY | FRIDAY | SATURDAY | SUNDAY | MOOD |
|---|---|---|---|---|---|---|---|---|---|
| 100 | | | | | | | | | |
| 75 | | | | | | | | | |
| 50 | | | | | | | | | |
| 25 | | | | | | | | | |
| 0 | | | | | | | | | |

This is my first log week.

# PRACTICAL STRATEGIES FOR DISOCCIATION

**WHAT SITUATIONS DO YOU FIND TRIGGERING OR EXACERBATE YOUR DEPERSONALIZATION/DEREALIZATION?**

_____
_____
_____
_____
_____

**WHAT FEATURES DO THESE SCENARIOS SHARE? ARE THEY STRESSFUL? UPSETTING? RANDOM? INVOLVE FAMILY? PAST TRAUMA?**

_____
_____
_____
_____
_____

**HOW DO YOU FEEL DURING THESE EVENTS? WHAT ARE YOU SYMPTOMS AND EMOTIONS, AND WHAT ARE YOUR THOUGHTS ON THEM?**

_____
_____
_____
_____
_____

**HOW CAN YOU PREPARE FOR THESE SITUATIONS IN THE FUTURE?**

_____
_____
_____
_____

**WHAT CHANGES CAN I MAKE TO IMPROVE MY SYMPTOMS AND FEELINGS DURING (OR AFTER) THESE SYMPTOMS? (E.G. GROUNDING TECHNIQUES, CHANGING THOUGHT PATTERNS, CALMING RITUALS, LOWER STRESS LEVELS DURING SOCIAL SITUATIONS ETC)**

_____
_____
_____
_____
_____

# TIME OF DAY ANXIETY & MOOD TRACKER

TRACK YOUR ANXIETY FLUCTUATIONS THROUGHOUT THE DAY TO SPOT POSSIBLE
TRIGGERS AND PATTERNS TO MANAGE YOUR STRESS/ANXIETY LEVELS MORE
EFFECTIVELY. WRITE TRIGGERS AND COPING MECHANISMS IN THE NOTES.

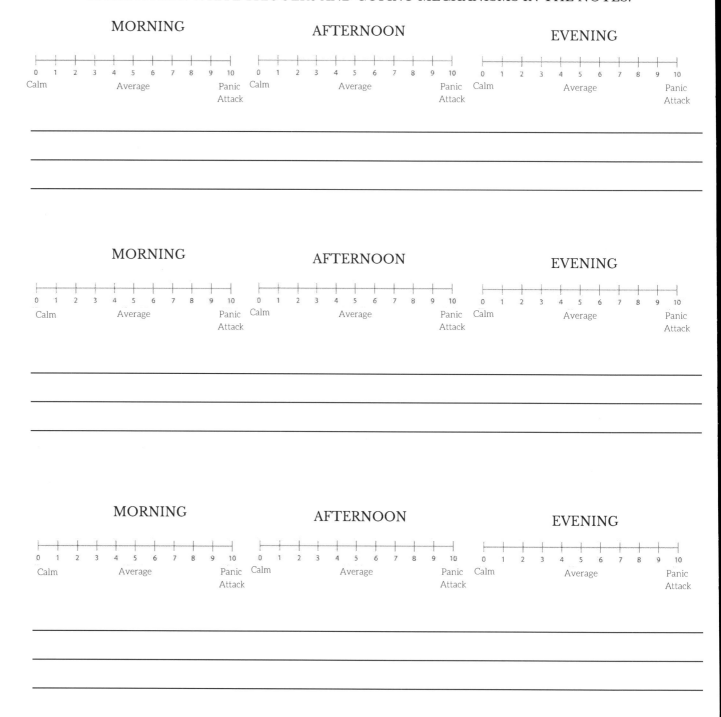

# GENERALIZED ANXIETY OVERVIEW WORKSHEET

WHAT SITUATIONS MAKE ME FEEL ANXIOUS?

_____
_____
_____
_____

WHAT THOUGHTS DO I HAVE DURING EPISODES OF ANXIETY?
(TAKE A NOTE OF NEGATIVE THOUGHTS ABOUT YOURSELF AND YOUR ABILITY TO HANDLE THE SITUATION)

_____
_____
_____
_____

IS THERE ANYTHING FLAWED IN MY THINKING DURING THESE EPISODES?

_____
_____
_____
_____

WHAT IS THE REALITY OF THE SITUATION AND WHAT CAN I THINK INSTEAD?

_____
_____
_____
_____

WHAT CHANGES CAN I MAKE TO IMPROVE MY ANXIETY DURING THIS SITUATION?
(E.G. CHANGING THOUGHT PATTERNS, CALMING RITUALS TO LOWER STRESS LEVELS
DURING SITUATIONS ETC)

_____
_____
_____
_____

# SLEEP TRACKER

| TOTAL SLEEP TIME | SLEEP START TIME | WAKE UP TIME | NAP TIMES | DATE |
|---|---|---|---|---|
|  |  |  |  |  |
|  |  |  |  |  |
|  |  |  |  |  |
|  |  |  |  |  |
|  |  |  |  |  |
|  |  |  |  |  |
|  |  |  |  |  |
|  |  |  |  |  |
|  |  |  |  |  |
|  |  |  |  |  |
|  |  |  |  |  |

# SYMPTOM TRACKER

| DATE | TIME | DURATION | DESCRIPTION |
|------|------|----------|-------------|
|      |      |          |             |
|      |      |          |             |
|      |      |          |             |
|      |      |          |             |
|      |      |          |             |
|      |      |          |             |
|      |      |          |             |
|      |      |          |             |
|      |      |          |             |
|      |      |          |             |
|      |      |          |             |
|      |      |          |             |
|      |      |          |             |
|      |      |          |             |
|      |      |          |             |
|      |      |          |             |
|      |      |          |             |
|      |      |          |             |
|      |      |          |             |
|      |      |          |             |
|      |      |          |             |
|      |      |          |             |
|      |      |          |             |
|      |      |          |             |
|      |      |          |             |
|      |      |          |             |
|      |      |          |             |
|      |      |          |             |
|      |      |          |             |
|      |      |          |             |
|      |      |          |             |
|      |      |          |             |

# WHEN IS GRATITUDE IMPORTANT?

ANSWER THESE QUESTIONS TO BREAK OUT OF NEGATIVE
THOUGHT PATTERNS AND REFOCUS ON THE THINGS THAT MAKE
YOU HAPPY AND GRATEFUL.

# DAILY ENERGY vs MOOD TRACKER

TRACK YOUR DAILY ENERGY AND MOOD USING DIFFERENT COLOURS ON THIS LINE CHART - NOTE YOUR TRIGGERS BELOW.

100

75

50

25

0

| MONDAY | TUESDAY | WEDNESDAY | THURSDAY | FRIDAY | SATURDAY | SUNDAY |
|--------|---------|-----------|----------|--------|----------|--------|

ENERGY

MOOD

# DEREALIZATION DEPERSONALIZATION DISORDER MENTAL HEALTH AND SYMPTOM CHECK LIST
PUT TIME STAMP, Y/N OR 0-5 FOR SEVERITY

| | FREQ. / SEVERITY Y/N | MON | TUES | WED | THURS | FRI | SAT | SUN |
|---|---|---|---|---|---|---|---|---|
| OVERALL MOOD | 0-5 | | | | | | | |
| ENERGY LEVELS | 0-5 | | | | | | | |
| ANXIETY | 0-5 | | | | | | | |
| AMNESIA / MEMORY PROBLEMS | 0-5 | | | | | | | |
| FEELING DETACHED FROM THOUGHTS | Y/N | | | | | | | |
| FEELING DETACHED/ OUTSIDE FROM BODY | Y/N | | | | | | | |
| THINGS FEELING "UNREAL" OR "DREAM LIKE" | Y/N | | | | | | | |
| DEPRESSION | Y/N | | | | | | | |
| EMOTIONAL NUMBNESS | Y/N | | | | | | | |
| RAPID CYCLING MOOD SWINGS | Y/N | | | | | | | |
| FEELING OVERWHELMED | 0-5 | | | | | | | |
| EXPERIENCED FLASHBACKS | Y/N | | | | | | | |
| SENSORY CHANGES E.G. TASTE, SMELL | Y/N | | | | | | | |
| LACK OF MOTIVATION | 0-5 | | | | | | | |
| ATTENDED THERAPY | Y/N | | | | | | | |
| TROUBLE SLEEPING | 0-5 | | | | | | | |
| SELF-CARE ACTIVITIES | Y/N | | | | | | | |
| LOGGED DIARY | Y/N | | | | | | | |
| VISUALS: OBJECTS FURTHER AWAY OR CLOSER | 0-5 | | | | | | | |
| VISUALS: VIVID COLOURS OR BRIGHTNESS | Y/N | | | | | | | |
| AUDIO PERCEPTION PROBLEMS E.G. ALTERED VOICE | 0-5 | | | | | | | |
| ENGAGED IN SOCIAL ACTIVITIES | Y/N | | | | | | | |
| SELF ESTEEM | 0-5 | | | | | | | |
| USED COPING SKILLS | Y/N | | | | | | | |

USE THIS CHART TO TRACK DAILY MOODS, SYMPTOMS AND HABITS. KEEP AN EYE IF THINGS CHANGE AND HOW YOU FEEL AFTER MAKING POSITIVE STEPS.

# DEREALIZATION DEPERSONALIZATION DISORDER MENTAL HEALTH AND SYMPTOM CHECK LIST
PUT TIME STAMP, Y/N or 0-5 FOR SEVERITY

| | FREQ. / SEVERITY Y/N | MON | TUES | WED | THURS | FRI | SAT | SUN |
|---|---|---|---|---|---|---|---|---|
| RELATIONSHIP PROBLEMS | Y/N | | | | | | | |
| OVERSLEEPING | 0-5 | | | | | | | |
| FEELING ON AUTOPILOT OR ROBOT | 0-5 | | | | | | | |
| GOING BLANK | 0-5 | | | | | | | |
| PANIC ATTACKS | Y/N | | | | | | | |
| FEELING FEARFUL | Y/N | | | | | | | |
| FEELING AS IF YOU ARE NOT REAL | Y/N | | | | | | | |
| FEELING TIME SLOWED DOWN OR SPED UP | Y/N | | | | | | | |
| FEELING PARALYSIS UNABLE TO MOVE | Y/N | | | | | | | |
| PEOPLE SEEM UNFAMILIAR | Y/N | | | | | | | |
| ENVIRONMENTS SEEM UNFAMILIAR | 0-5 | | | | | | | |
| OBSERVING INTERNAL SENSATIONS | Y/N | | | | | | | |
| FEELING FOGGY | Y/N | | | | | | | |
| OVERTHINKING | 0-5 | | | | | | | |
| CONFUSION | Y/N | | | | | | | |
| DISORGANISATION | 0-5 | | | | | | | |
| DIFFICULTY CONCENTRATING | Y/N | | | | | | | |
| DIFFICULTY COMPLETING TASKS | Y/N | | | | | | | |
| FEELING IRRITABLE | 0-5 | | | | | | | |
| EXPERIENCED RELATIONSHIP PROBLEMS | Y/N | | | | | | | |
| FEELING DETACHED | 0-5 | | | | | | | |
| DECREASED SENSATIONS | Y/N | | | | | | | |
| CONSUMED ALCOHOL | 0-5 | | | | | | | |
| CONSUMED RECREATIONAL DRUGS | Y/N | | | | | | | |

USE THIS CHART TO TRACK DAILY MOODS, SYMPTOMS AND HABITS. KEEP AN EYE IF THINGS CHANGE AND HOW YOU FEEL AFTER MAKING POSITIVE STEPS.

| | FREQ. / SEVERITY Y/N | MON | TUES | WED | THURS | FRI | SAT | SUN |
|---|---|---|---|---|---|---|---|---|
| EXERCISE | MINS | | | | | | | |
| FEELING CALM | 0-5 | | | | | | | |
| FEELING HAPPY | 0-5 | | | | | | | |
| FEELING PRODUCTIVE | 0-5 | | | | | | | |
| WORK/SCHOOL STRESS | 0-5 | | | | | | | |
| GENERAL STRESS | 0-5 | | | | | | | |
| SPOKE TO SOMEONE ABOUT FEELINGS | Y/N | | | | | | | |
| MEDICATION | DOSE | | | | | | | |
| MEDICATION | DOSE | | | | | | | |
| MEDICATION | DOSE | | | | | | | |
| MEDICATION | DOSE | | | | | | | |
| MEDICATION | DOSE | | | | | | | |

FILL IN THE CHARTS TO TRACK EVENTS, MOODS, TRIGGERS, THINGS YOU WANT TO CHANGE, DETAILED NOTES

_____
_____
_____
_____
_____
_____
_____
_____
_____
_____
_____
_____
_____

HOW OFTEN WAS THIS CHART FILLED OUT?
NOT AT ALL    [ ]        1-3X PER WEEK    [ ]        ALMOST EVERY DAY    [ ]        EVERYDAY  [ ]

# TIME OF DAY SYMPTOM TRACKER

TRACK THE SEVERITY OF YOUR SYMPTOMS THROUGHOUT THE DAY USING THE SCALE, USE THE NOTE SECTION BELOW TO LIST THE SYMPTOMS YOU EXPERIENCED. USE THIS TO SEE IF CERTAIN TIMES OF DAY E.G. MEAL TIMES OR FIRST THING IN THE MORNING, ARE TRIGGERS FOR YOU.

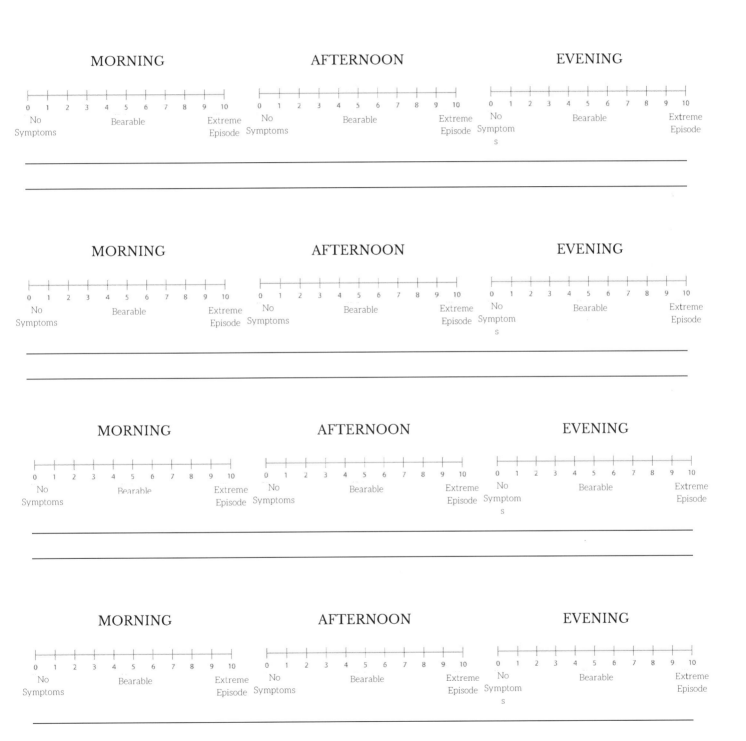

# GROUNDING TECHNIQUES

**WHAT CAN YOU SEE AROUND YOU? WHO OR WHAT SEEMS FAMILIAR? OR DESCRIBE A CALMING PLACE AND WHAT IT LOOKS LIKE.**

**TRY LISTENING TO THE SOUNDS AROUND YOU OR GO SOMEWHERE WITH FAMILIAR CALMING SOUNDS E.G. SOUNDS OF NATURE OR A FAVOURITE SONG. DESCRIBE THOSE SOUNDS.**

**USING ALL YOUR SENSES LIKE SMELL, TASTE, TOUCH, HEARING, DESCRIBE YOUR SURROUNDINGS OR YOUR FAVOURITE EXPERIENCES E.G. FAVOURITE FOOD.**

**HOW DO YOU CURRENTLY FEEL? AND WHAT DO YOU THINK ABOUT HOW YOU CURRENTLY FEEL? CAN YOU CHALLENGE THOSE THOUGHTS?**

**WHAT IS YOUR PREFERRED GROUNDING TECHNIQUE? E.G. BREATHING SLOWLY? DISTRACTING YOURSELF? MAKE A LIST OF TECHNIQUES YOU CAN USE WHEN YOU FEEL YOUR SYMPTOMS ARE BAD OR YOUR ANXIETY OR MOOD AROUND THEM ARE TROUBLING YOU.**

# PRACTICAL STRATEGIES FOR DISOCCIATION

TRIGGER WARNING:
WHAT MAY HELP ONE PERSON MAY TRIGGER OTHERS, USE THESE TECHNIQUES WITH CAUTION AND MODIFY THEM AROUND YOU.

## WHAT SITUATIONS DO YOU FIND TRIGGERING OR EXACERBATE YOUR DEPERSONALIZATION/DEREALIZATION?

## WHAT FEATURES DO THESE SCENARIOS SHARE? ARE THEY STRESSFUL? UPSETTING? RANDOM? INVOLVE FAMILY? PAST TRAUMA?

## HOW DO YOU FEEL DURING THESE EVENTS? WHAT ARE YOU SYMPTOMS AND EMOTIONS, AND WHAT ARE YOUR THOUGHTS ON THEM?

## HOW CAN YOU PREPARE FOR THESE SITUATIONS IN THE FUTURE?

## WHAT CHANGES CAN I MAKE TO IMPROVE MY SYMPTOMS AND FEELINGS DURING (OR AFTER) THESE SYMPTOMS? (E.G. GROUNDING TECHNIQUES, CHANGING THOUGHT PATTERNS, CALMING RITUALS TO LOWER STRESS LEVELS DURING SOCIAL SITUATIONS ETC)

# TIME OF DAY ANXIETY & MOOD TRACKER

TRACK YOUR ANXIETY FLUCTUATIONS THROUGHOUT THE DAY TO SPOT POSSIBLE
TRIGGERS AND PATTERNS TO MANAGE YOUR STRESS/ANXIETY LEVELS MORE
EFFECTIVELY. WRITE TRIGGERS AND COPING MECHANISMS IN THE NOTES.

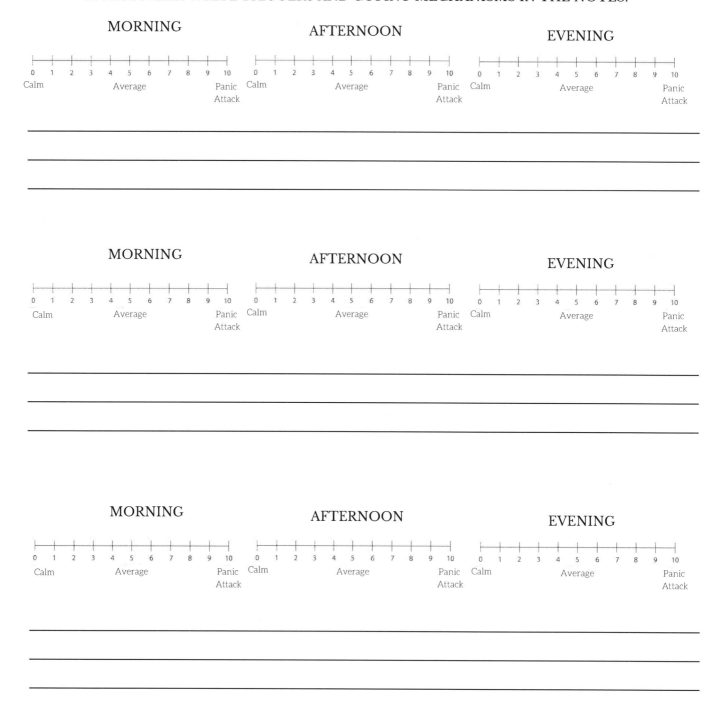

### MORNING

```
0  1  2  3  4  5  6  7  8  9  10
Calm          Average          Panic
                                Attack
```

### AFTERNOON

```
0  1  2  3  4  5  6  7  8  9  10
Calm          Average          Panic
                                Attack
```

### EVENING

```
0  1  2  3  4  5  6  7  8  9  10
Calm          Average          Panic
                                Attack
```

---

### MORNING

```
0  1  2  3  4  5  6  7  8  9  10
Calm          Average          Panic
                                Attack
```

### AFTERNOON

```
0  1  2  3  4  5  6  7  8  9  10
Calm          Average          Panic
                                Attack
```

### EVENING

```
0  1  2  3  4  5  6  7  8  9  10
Calm          Average          Panic
                                Attack
```

---

### MORNING

```
0  1  2  3  4  5  6  7  8  9  10
Calm          Average          Panic
                                Attack
```

### AFTERNOON

```
0  1  2  3  4  5  6  7  8  9  10
Calm          Average          Panic
                                Attack
```

### EVENING

```
0  1  2  3  4  5  6  7  8  9  10
Calm          Average          Panic
                                Attack
```

# GENERALIZED ANXIETY OVERVIEW WORKSHEET

WHAT SITUATIONS MAKE ME FEEL ANXIOUS?

_____

_____

_____

_____

WHAT THOUGHTS DO I HAVE DURING EPISODES OF ANXIETY?
(TAKE A NOTE OF NEGATIVE THOUGHTS ABOUT YOURSELF AND YOUR ABILITY TO HANDLE THE SITUATION)

_____

_____

_____

_____

IS THERE ANYTHING FLAWED IN MY THINKING DURING THESE EPISODES?

_____

_____

_____

_____

WHAT IS THE REALITY OF THE SITUATION AND WHAT CAN I THINK INSTEAD?

_____

_____

_____

WHAT CHANGES CAN I MAKE TO IMPROVE MY ANXIETY DURING THIS SITUATION?
(E.G. CHANGING THOUGHT PATTERNS, CALMING RITUALS TO LOWER STRESS LEVELS
DURING SITUATIONS ETC)

_____

_____

_____

# SLEEP TRACKER

| TOTAL SLEEP TIME | SLEEP START TIME | WAKE UP TIME | NAP TIMES | DATE |
|---|---|---|---|---|
| | | | | |
| | | | | |
| | | | | |
| | | | | |
| | | | | |
| | | | | |
| | | | | |
| | | | | |
| | | | | |
| | | | | |
| | | | | |
| | | | | |

# SYMPTOM TRACKER

| DATE | TIME | DURATION | DESCRIPTION |
|------|------|----------|-------------|
|      |      |          |             |
|      |      |          |             |
|      |      |          |             |
|      |      |          |             |
|      |      |          |             |
|      |      |          |             |
|      |      |          |             |
|      |      |          |             |
|      |      |          |             |
|      |      |          |             |
|      |      |          |             |
|      |      |          |             |
|      |      |          |             |
|      |      |          |             |
|      |      |          |             |
|      |      |          |             |
|      |      |          |             |
|      |      |          |             |
|      |      |          |             |
|      |      |          |             |
|      |      |          |             |
|      |      |          |             |
|      |      |          |             |
|      |      |          |             |
|      |      |          |             |
|      |      |          |             |
|      |      |          |             |
|      |      |          |             |
|      |      |          |             |
|      |      |          |             |
|      |      |          |             |
|      |      |          |             |

# WHO ARE YOU MOST GRATEFUL FOR?

ANSWER THESE QUESTIONS TO BREAK OUT OF NEGATIVE
THOUGHT PATTERNS AND REFOCUS ON THE THINGS THAT MAKE
YOU HAPPY AND GRATEFUL.

# DAILY ENERGY vs MOOD TRACKER

TRACK YOUR DAILY ENERGY AND MOOD USING DIFFERENT COLOURS ON THIS LINE CHART - NOTE YOUR TRIGGERS BELOW.

100

75

50

25

0

ENERGY   MONDAY   TUESDAY   WEDNESDAY   THURSDAY   FRIDAY   SATURDAY   SUNDAY

MOOD

# DEREALIZATION DEPERSONALIZATION DISORDER MENTAL HEALTH AND SYMPTOM CHECK LIST
PUT TIME STAMP, Y/N OR 0-5 FOR SEVERITY

| | FREQ. / SEVERITY Y/N | MON | TUES | WED | THURS | FRI | SAT | SUN |
|---|---|---|---|---|---|---|---|---|
| OVERALL MOOD | 0-5 | | | | | | | |
| ENERGY LEVELS | 0-5 | | | | | | | |
| ANXIETY | 0-5 | | | | | | | |
| AMNESIA / MEMORY PROBLEMS | 0-5 | | | | | | | |
| FEELING DETACHED FROM THOUGHTS | Y/N | | | | | | | |
| FEELING DETACHED/ OUTSIDE FROM BODY | Y/N | | | | | | | |
| THINGS FEELING "UNREAL" OR "DREAM LIKE" | Y/N | | | | | | | |
| DEPRESSION | Y/N | | | | | | | |
| EMOTIONAL NUMBNESS | Y/N | | | | | | | |
| RAPID CYCLING MOOD SWINGS | Y/N | | | | | | | |
| FEELING OVERWHELMED | 0-5 | | | | | | | |
| EXPERIENCED FLASHBACKS | Y/N | | | | | | | |
| SENSORY CHANGES E.G. TASTE, SMELL | Y/N | | | | | | | |
| LACK OF MOTIVATION | 0-5 | | | | | | | |
| ATTENDED THERAPY | Y/N | | | | | | | |
| TROUBLE SLEEPING | 0-5 | | | | | | | |
| SELF-CARE ACTIVITIES | Y/N | | | | | | | |
| LOGGED DIARY | Y/N | | | | | | | |
| VISUALS: OBJECTS FURTHER AWAY OR CLOSER | 0-5 | | | | | | | |
| VISUALS: VIVID COLOURS OR BRIGHTNESS | Y/N | | | | | | | |
| AUDIO PERCEPTION PROBLEMS E.G. ALTERED VOICE | 0-5 | | | | | | | |
| ENGAGED IN SOCIAL ACTIVITIES | Y/N | | | | | | | |
| SELF ESTEEM | 0-5 | | | | | | | |
| USED COPING SKILLS | Y/N | | | | | | | |

USE THIS CHART TO TRACK DAILY MOODS, SYMPTOMS AND HABITS. KEEP AN EYE IF THINGS CHANGE AND HOW YOU FEEL AFTER MAKING POSITIVE STEPS.

# DEREALIZATION DEPERSONALIZATION DISORDER MENTAL HEALTH AND SYMPTOM CHECK LIST
## PUT TIME STAMP,Y/N OR 0-5 FOR SEVERITY

| | FREQ. / SEVERITY Y/N | MON | TUES | WED | THURS | FRI | SAT | SUN |
|---|---|---|---|---|---|---|---|---|
| RELATIONSHIP PROBLEMS | Y/N | | | | | | | |
| OVERSLEEPING | 0-5 | | | | | | | |
| FEELING ON AUTOPILOT OR ROBOT | 0-5 | | | | | | | |
| GOING BLANK | 0-5 | | | | | | | |
| PANIC ATTACKS | Y/N | | | | | | | |
| FEELING FEARFUL | Y/N | | | | | | | |
| FEELING AS IF YOU ARE NOT REAL | Y/N | | | | | | | |
| FEELING TIME SLOWED DOWN OR SPED UP | Y/N | | | | | | | |
| FEELING PARALYSIS UNABLE TO MOVE | Y/N | | | | | | | |
| PEOPLE SEEM UNFAMILIAR | Y/N | | | | | | | |
| ENVIRONMENTS SEEM UNFAMILIAR | 0-5 | | | | | | | |
| OBSERVING INTERNAL SENSATIONS | Y/N | | | | | | | |
| FEELING FOGGY | Y/N | | | | | | | |
| OVERTHINKING | 0-5 | | | | | | | |
| CONFUSION | Y/N | | | | | | | |
| DISORGANISATION | 0-5 | | | | | | | |
| DIFFICULTY CONCENTRATING | Y/N | | | | | | | |
| DIFFICULTY COMPLETING TASKS | Y/N | | | | | | | |
| FEELING IRRITABLE | 0-5 | | | | | | | |
| EXPERIENCED RELATIONSHIP PROBLEMS | Y/N | | | | | | | |
| FEELING DETACHED | 0-5 | | | | | | | |
| DECREASED SENSATIONS | Y/N | | | | | | | |
| CONSUMED ALCOHOL | 0-5 | | | | | | | |
| CONSUMED RECREATIONAL DRUGS | Y/N | | | | | | | |

USE THIS CHART TO TRACK DAILY MOODS, SYMPTOMS AND HABITS. KEEP AN EYE IF THINGS CHANGE AND HOW YOU FEEL AFTER MAKING POSITIVE STEPS.

| | FREQ. / SEVERITY Y/N | MON | TUES | WED | THURS | FRI | SAT | SUN |
|---|---|---|---|---|---|---|---|---|
| EXERCISE | MINS | | | | | | | |
| FEELING CALM | 0-5 | | | | | | | |
| FEELING HAPPY | 0-5 | | | | | | | |
| FEELING PRODUCTIVE | 0-5 | | | | | | | |
| WORK/SCHOOL STRESS | 0-5 | | | | | | | |
| GENERAL STRESS | 0-5 | | | | | | | |
| SPOKE TO SOMEONE ABOUT FEELINGS | Y/N | | | | | | | |
| MEDICATION | DOSE | | | | | | | |
| MEDICATION | DOSE | | | | | | | |
| MEDICATION | DOSE | | | | | | | |
| MEDICATION | DOSE | | | | | | | |
| MEDICATION | DOSE | | | | | | | |

FILL IN THE CHARTS TO TRACK EVENTS, MOODS, TRIGGERS, THINGS YOU WANT TO CHANGE, DETAILED NOTES

_____
_____
_____
_____
_____
_____
_____
_____
_____
_____
_____
_____
_____
_____

## HOW OFTEN WAS THIS CHART FILLED OUT?

NOT AT ALL   [ ]          1-3X PER WEEK   [ ]          ALMOST EVERY DAY   [ ]          EVERYDAY   [ ]

# TIME OF DAY SYMPTOM TRACKER

TRACK THE SEVERITY OF YOUR SYMPTOMS THROUGHOUT THE DAY USING THE SCALE, USE THE NOTE SECTION BELOW TO LIST THE SYMPTOMS YOU EXPERIENCED. USE THIS TO SEE IF CERTAIN TIMES OF DAY E.G. MEAL TIMES OR FIRST THING IN THE MORNING, ARE TRIGGERS FOR YOU.

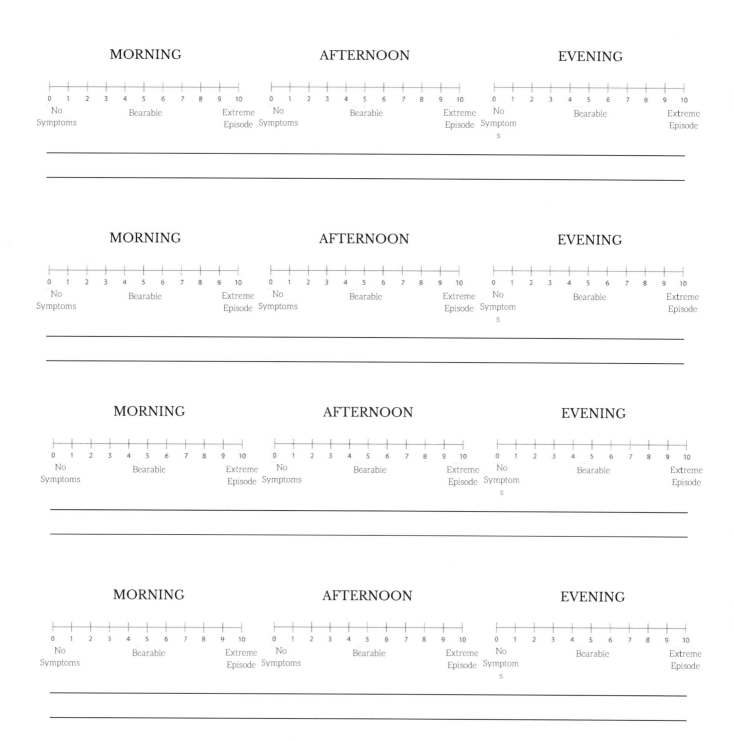

# GROUNDING TECHNIQUES

**WHAT CAN YOU SEE AROUND YOU? WHO OR WHAT SEEMS FAMILIAR? OR DESCRIBE A CALMING PLACE AND WHAT IT LOOKS LIKE.**

---

---

---

---

**TRY LISTENING TO THE SOUNDS AROUND YOU OR GO SOMEWHERE WITH FAMILIAR CALMING SOUNDS E.G. SOUNDS OF NATURE OR A FAVOURITE SONG. DESCRIBE THOSE SOUNDS.**

---

---

---

---

**USING ALL YOUR SENSES LIKE SMELL, TASTE, TOUCH, HEARING, DESCRIBE YOUR SURROUNDINGS OR YOUR FAVOURITE EXPERIENCES E.G. FAVOURITE FOOD.**

---

---

---

---

**HOW DO YOU CURRENTLY FEEL? AND WHAT DO YOU THINK ABOUT HOW YOU CURRENTLY FEEL? CAN YOU CHALLENGE THOSE THOUGHTS?**

---

---

---

---

**WHAT IS YOUR PREFERRED GROUNDING TECHNIQUE? E.G. BREATHING SLOWLY? DISTRACTING YOURSELF? MAKE A LIST OF TECHNIQUES YOU CAN USE WHEN YOU FEEL YOUR SYMPTOMS ARE BAD OR YOUR ANXIETY OR MOOD AROUND THEM ARE TROUBLING YOU.**

---

---

---

---

# PRACTICAL STRATEGIES FOR DISOCCIATION

TRIGGER WARNING:
WHAT MAY HELP ONE PERSON MAY TRIGGER OTHERS, USE THESE TECHNIQUES WITH CAUTION AND MODIFY THEM AROUND YOU.

## WHAT SITUATIONS DO YOU FIND TRIGGERING OR EXACERBATE YOUR DEPERSONALIZATION/DEREALIZATION?

_____

_____

_____

_____

_____

## WHAT FEATURES DO THESE SCENARIOS SHARE? ARE THEY STRESSFUL? UPSETTING? RANDOM? INVOLVE FAMILY? PAST TRAUMA?

_____

_____

_____

_____

_____

## HOW DO YOU FEEL DURING THESE EVENTS? WHAT ARE YOU SYMPTOMS AND EMOTIONS, AND WHAT ARE YOUR THOUGHTS ON THEM?

_____

_____

_____

_____

## HOW CAN YOU PREPARE FOR THESE SITUATIONS IN THE FUTURE?

_____

_____

_____

_____

## WHAT CHANGES CAN I MAKE TO IMPROVE MY SYMPTOMS AND FEELINGS DURING (OR AFTER) THESE SYMPTOMS? (E.G. GROUNDING TECHNIQUES, CHANGING THOUGHT PATTERNS, CALMING RITUALS TO LOWER STRESS LEVELS DURING SOCIAL SITUATIONS ETC)

_____

_____

_____

_____

# TIME OF DAY ANXIETY & MOOD TRACKER

TRACK YOUR ANXIETY FLUCTUATIONS THROUGHOUT THE DAY TO SPOT POSSIBLE
TRIGGERS AND PATTERNS TO MANAGE YOUR STRESS/ANXIETY LEVELS MORE
EFFECTIVELY. WRITE TRIGGERS AND COPING MECHANISMS IN THE NOTES.

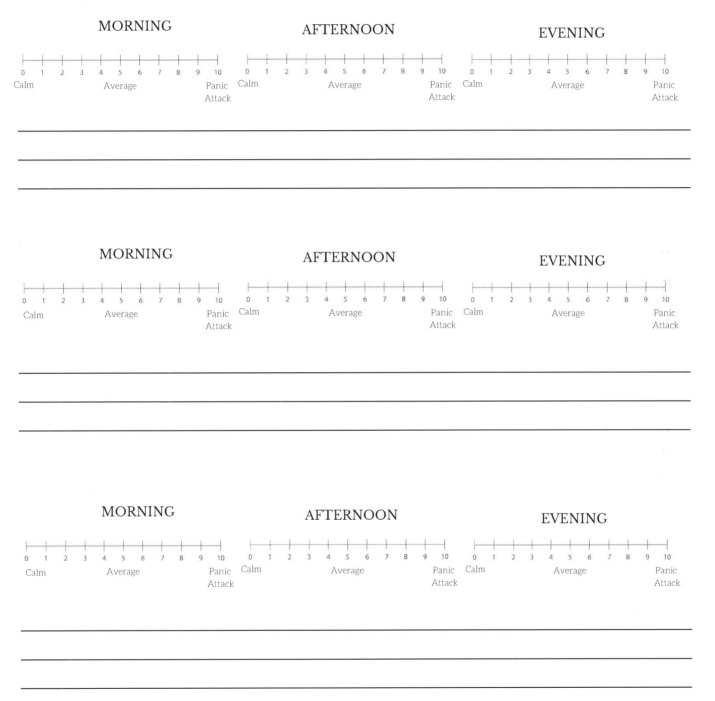

# GENERALIZED ANXIETY OVERVIEW WORKSHEET

WHAT SITUATIONS MAKE ME FEEL ANXIOUS?

_____
_____
_____
_____
_____

WHAT THOUGHTS DO I HAVE DURING EPISODES OF ANXIETY?
(TAKE A NOTE OF NEGATIVE THOUGHTS ABOUT YOURSELF AND YOUR ABILITY TO HANDLE THE SITUATION)

_____
_____
_____
_____
_____

IS THERE ANYTHING FLAWED IN MY THINKING DURING THESE EPISODES?

_____
_____
_____
_____
_____

WHAT IS THE REALITY OF THE SITUATION AND WHAT CAN I THINK INSTEAD?

_____
_____
_____
_____
_____

WHAT CHANGES CAN I MAKE TO IMPROVE MY ANXIETY DURING THIS SITUATION?
(E.G. CHANGING THOUGHT PATTERNS, CALMING RITUALS TO LOWER STRESS LEVELS
DURING SITUATIONS ETC)

_____
_____
_____
_____
_____

# SLEEP TRACKER

| TOTAL SLEEP TIME | SLEEP START TIME | WAKE UP TIME | NAP TIMES | DATE |
|---|---|---|---|---|
| | | | | |
| | | | | |
| | | | | |
| | | | | |
| | | | | |
| | | | | |
| | | | | |
| | | | | |
| | | | | |
| | | | | |
| | | | | |

# SYMPTOM TRACKER

| DATE | TIME | DURATION | DESCRIPTION |
|------|------|----------|-------------|
|      |      |          |             |
|      |      |          |             |
|      |      |          |             |
|      |      |          |             |
|      |      |          |             |
|      |      |          |             |
|      |      |          |             |
|      |      |          |             |
|      |      |          |             |
|      |      |          |             |
|      |      |          |             |
|      |      |          |             |
|      |      |          |             |
|      |      |          |             |
|      |      |          |             |
|      |      |          |             |
|      |      |          |             |
|      |      |          |             |
|      |      |          |             |
|      |      |          |             |
|      |      |          |             |
|      |      |          |             |
|      |      |          |             |
|      |      |          |             |
|      |      |          |             |
|      |      |          |             |
|      |      |          |             |
|      |      |          |             |
|      |      |          |             |
|      |      |          |             |
|      |      |          |             |
|      |      |          |             |

# DAILY ENERGY  vs MOOD TRACKER

TRACK YOUR DAILY ENERGY AND MOOD USING DIFFERENT COLOURS ON THIS LINE CHART - NOTE YOUR TRIGGERS BELOW.

100

75

50

25

0

ENERGY

| MONDAY | TUESDAY | WEDNESDAY | THURSDAY | FRIDAY | SATURDAY | SUNDAY |
|--------|---------|-----------|----------|--------|----------|--------|

MOOD

# DEREALIZATION DEPERSONALIZATION DISORDER MENTAL HEALTH AND SYMPTOM CHECK LIST
## PUT TIME STAMP, Y/N OR 0-5 FOR SEVERITY

| | FREQ. / SEVERITY Y/N | MON | TUES | WED | THURS | FRI | SAT | SUN |
|---|---|---|---|---|---|---|---|---|
| OVERALL MOOD | 0-5 | | | | | | | |
| ENERGY LEVELS | 0-5 | | | | | | | |
| ANXIETY | 0-5 | | | | | | | |
| AMNESIA / MEMORY PROBLEMS | 0-5 | | | | | | | |
| FEELING DETACHED FROM THOUGHTS | Y/N | | | | | | | |
| FEELING DETACHED/ OUTSIDE FROM BODY | Y/N | | | | | | | |
| THINGS FEELING "UNREAL" OR "DREAM LIKE" | Y/N | | | | | | | |
| DEPRESSION | Y/N | | | | | | | |
| EMOTIONAL NUMBNESS | Y/N | | | | | | | |
| RAPID CYCLING MOOD SWINGS | Y/N | | | | | | | |
| FEELING OVERWHELMED | 0-5 | | | | | | | |
| EXPERIENCED FLASHBACKS | Y/N | | | | | | | |
| SENSORY CHANGES E.G. TASTE, SMELL | Y/N | | | | | | | |
| LACK OF MOTIVATION | 0-5 | | | | | | | |
| ATTENDED THERAPY | Y/N | | | | | | | |
| TROUBLE SLEEPING | 0-5 | | | | | | | |
| SELF-CARE ACTIVITIES | Y/N | | | | | | | |
| LOGGED DIARY | Y/N | | | | | | | |
| VISUALS: OBJECTS FURTHER AWAY OR CLOSER | 0-5 | | | | | | | |
| VISUALS: VIVID COLOURS OR BRIGHTNESS | Y/N | | | | | | | |
| AUDIO PERCEPTION PROBLEMS E.G. ALTERED VOICE | 0-5 | | | | | | | |
| ENGAGED IN SOCIAL ACTIVITIES | Y/N | | | | | | | |
| SELF ESTEEM | 0-5 | | | | | | | |
| USED COPING SKILLS | Y/N | | | | | | | |

USE THIS CHART TO TRACK DAILY MOODS, SYMPTOMS AND HABITS. KEEP AN EYE IF THINGS CHANGE AND HOW YOU FEEL AFTER MAKING POSITIVE STEPS.

# DEREALIZATION DEPERSONALIZATION DISORDER MENTAL HEALTH AND SYMPTOM CHECK LIST
## PUT TIME STAMP, Y/N OR 0-5 FOR SEVERITY

| | FREQ. / SEVERITY Y/N | MON | TUES | WED | THURS | FRI | SAT | SUN |
|---|---|---|---|---|---|---|---|---|
| RELATIONSHIP PROBLEMS | Y/N | | | | | | | |
| OVERSLEEPING | 0-5 | | | | | | | |
| FEELING ON AUTOPILOT OR ROBOT | 0-5 | | | | | | | |
| GOING BLANK | 0-5 | | | | | | | |
| PANIC ATTACKS | Y/N | | | | | | | |
| FEELING FEARFUL | Y/N | | | | | | | |
| FEELING AS IF YOU ARE NOT REAL | Y/N | | | | | | | |
| FEELING TIME SLOWED DOWN OR SPED UP | Y/N | | | | | | | |
| FEELING PARALYSIS UNABLE TO MOVE | Y/N | | | | | | | |
| PEOPLE SEEM UNFAMILIAR | Y/N | | | | | | | |
| ENVIRONMENTS SEEM UNFAMILIAR | 0-5 | | | | | | | |
| OBSERVING INTERNAL SENSATIONS | Y/N | | | | | | | |
| FEELING FOGGY | Y/N | | | | | | | |
| OVERTHINKING | 0-5 | | | | | | | |
| CONFUSION | Y/N | | | | | | | |
| DISORGANISATION | 0-5 | | | | | | | |
| DIFFICULTY CONCENTRATING | Y/N | | | | | | | |
| DIFFICULTY COMPLETING TASKS | Y/N | | | | | | | |
| FEELING IRRITABLE | 0-5 | | | | | | | |
| EXPERIENCED RELATIONSHIP PROBLEMS | Y/N | | | | | | | |
| FEELING DETACHED | 0-5 | | | | | | | |
| DECREASED SENSATIONS | Y/N | | | | | | | |
| CONSUMED ALCOHOL | 0-5 | | | | | | | |
| CONSUMED RECREATIONAL DRUGS | Y/N | | | | | | | |

USE THIS CHART TO TRACK DAILY MOODS, SYMPTOMS AND HABITS. KEEP AN EYE IF THINGS CHANGE AND HOW YOU FEEL AFTER MAKING POSITIVE STEPS.

| | FREQ. / SEVERITY Y/N | MON | TUES | WED | THURS | FRI | SAT | SUN |
|---|---|---|---|---|---|---|---|---|
| EXERCISE | MINS | | | | | | | |
| FEELING CALM | 0-5 | | | | | | | |
| FEELING HAPPY | 0-5 | | | | | | | |
| FEELING PRODUCTIVE | 0-5 | | | | | | | |
| WORK/SCHOOL STRESS | 0-5 | | | | | | | |
| GENERAL STRESS | 0-5 | | | | | | | |
| SPOKE TO SOMEONE ABOUT FEELINGS | Y/N | | | | | | | |
| MEDICATION | DOSE | | | | | | | |
| MEDICATION | DOSE | | | | | | | |
| MEDICATION | DOSE | | | | | | | |
| MEDICATION | DOSE | | | | | | | |
| MEDICATION | DOSE | | | | | | | |

FILL IN THE CHARTS TO TRACK EVENTS, MOODS, TRIGGERS, THINGS YOU WANT TO CHANGE, DETAILED NOTES

_____
_____
_____
_____
_____
_____
_____
_____
_____
_____
_____
_____
_____

HOW OFTEN WAS THIS CHART FILLED OUT?
NOT AT ALL    [ ]        1-3X PER WEEK    [ ]         ALMOST EVERY DAY    [ ]          EVERYDAY   [ ]

# TIME OF DAY SYMPTOM TRACKER

TRACK THE SEVERITY OF YOUR SYMPTOMS THROUGHOUT THE DAY USING THE
SCALE, USE THE NOTE SECTION BELOW TO LIST THE SYMPTOMS YOU EXPERIENCED.
USE THIS TO SEE IF CERTAIN TIMES OF DAY E.G. MEAL TIMES OR FIRST THING IN THE
MORNING, ARE TRIGGERS FOR YOU.

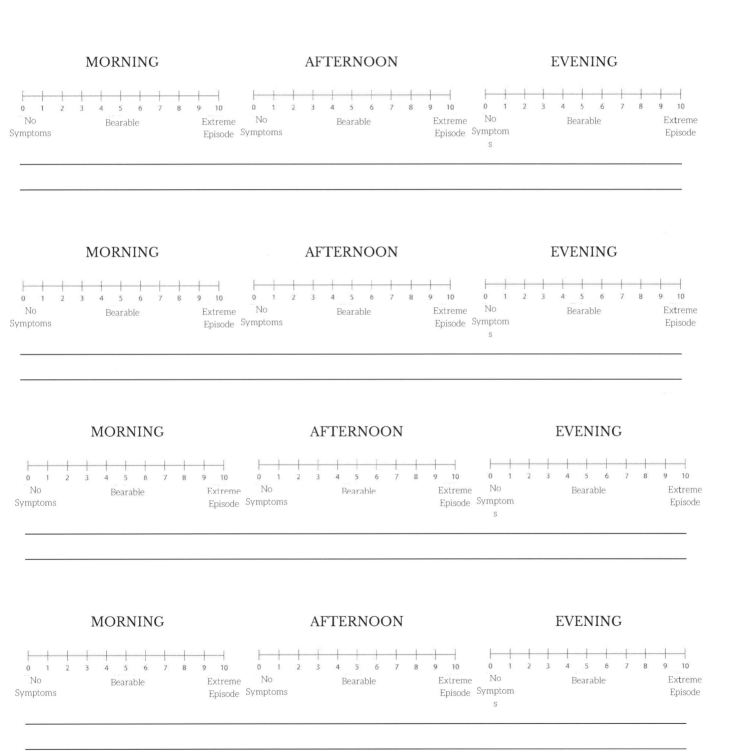

# GROUNDING TECHNIQUES

**WHAT CAN YOU SEE AROUND YOU? WHO OR WHAT SEEMS FAMILIAR? OR DESCRIBE A CALMING PLACE AND WHAT IT LOOKS LIKE.**

_____

_____

_____

_____

_____

**TRY LISTENING TO THE SOUNDS AROUND YOU OR GO SOMEWHERE WITH FAMILIAR CALMING SOUNDS E.G. SOUNDS OF NATURE OR A FAVOURITE SONG. DESCRIBE THOSE SOUNDS.**

_____

_____

_____

_____

_____

**USING ALL YOUR SENSES LIKE SMELL, TASTE, TOUCH, HEARING, DESCRIBE YOUR SURROUNDINGS OR YOUR FAVOURITE EXPERIENCES E.G. FAVOURITE FOOD.**

_____

_____

_____

_____

_____

**HOW DO YOU CURRENTLY FEEL? AND WHAT DO YOU THINK ABOUT HOW YOU CURRENTLY FEEL? CAN YOU CHALLENGE THOSE THOUGHTS?**

_____

_____

_____

_____

_____

**WHAT IS YOUR PREFERRED GROUNDING TECHNIQUE? E.G. BREATHING SLOWLY? DISTRACTING YOURSELF? MAKE A LIST OF TECHNIQUES YOU CAN USE WHEN YOU FEEL YOUR SYMPTOMS ARE BAD OR YOUR ANXIETY OR MOOD AROUND THEM ARE TROUBLING YOU.**

_____

_____

_____

_____

_____

# PRACTICAL STRATEGIES FOR DISOCCIATION

TRIGGER WARNING:
WHAT MAY HELP ONE PERSON MAY TRIGGER OTHERS, USE THESE TECHNIQUES WITH CAUTION AND MODIFY THEM AROUND YOU.

**WHAT SITUATIONS DO YOU FIND TRIGGERING OR EXACERBATE YOUR DEPERSONALIZATION/DEREALIZATION?**

_____

_____

_____

_____

_____

**WHAT FEATURES DO THESE SCENARIOS SHARE? ARE THEY STRESSFUL? UPSETTING? RANDOM? INVOLVE FAMILY? PAST TRAUMA?**

_____

_____

_____

_____

**HOW DO YOU FEEL DURING THESE EVENTS? WHAT ARE YOU SYMPTOMS AND EMOTIONS, AND WHAT ARE YOUR THOUGHTS ON THEM?**

_____

_____

_____

_____

**HOW CAN YOU PREPARE FOR THESE SITUATIONS IN THE FUTURE?**

_____

_____

_____

_____

**WHAT CHANGES CAN I MAKE TO IMPROVE MY SYMPTOMS AND FEELINGS DURING (OR AFTER) THESE SYMPTOMS? (E.G. GROUNDING TECHNIQUES, CHANGING THOUGHT PATTERNS, CALMING RITUALS TO LOWER STRESS LEVELS DURING SOCIAL SITUATIONS ETC)**

_____

_____

_____

_____

# TIME OF DAY ANXIETY & MOOD TRACKER

TRACK YOUR ANXIETY FLUCTUATIONS THROUGHOUT THE DAY TO SPOT POSSIBLE TRIGGERS AND PATTERNS TO MANAGE YOUR STRESS/ANXIETY LEVELS MORE EFFECTIVELY. WRITE TRIGGERS AND COPING MECHANISMS IN THE NOTES.

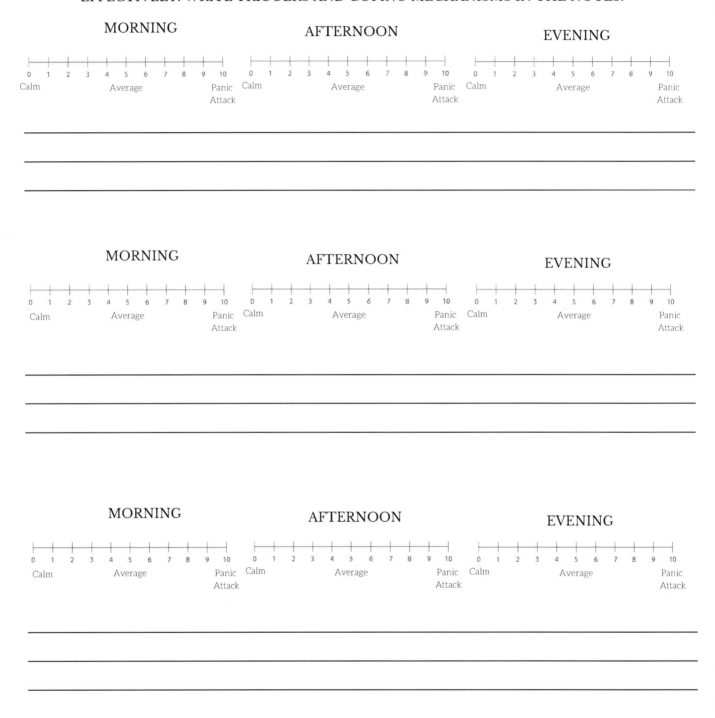

# GENERALIZED ANXIETY OVERVIEW WORKSHEET

WHAT SITUATIONS MAKE ME FEEL ANXIOUS?

_____
_____
_____
_____
_____

WHAT THOUGHTS DO I HAVE DURING EPISODES OF ANXIETY?
(TAKE A NOTE OF NEGATIVE THOUGHTS ABOUT YOURSELF AND YOUR ABILITY TO HANDLE THE SITUATION)

_____
_____
_____
_____

IS THERE ANYTHING FLAWED IN MY THINKING DURING THESE EPISODES?

_____
_____
_____
_____
_____

WHAT IS THE REALITY OF THE SITUATION AND WHAT CAN I THINK INSTEAD?

_____
_____
_____
_____

WHAT CHANGES CAN I MAKE TO IMPROVE MY ANXIETY DURING THIS SITUATION?
(E.G. CHANGING THOUGHT PATTERNS, CALMING RITUALS TO LOWER STRESS LEVELS
DURING SITUATIONS ETC)

_____
_____
_____
_____

# SLEEP TRACKER

| TOTAL SLEEP TIME | SLEEP START TIME | WAKE UP TIME | NAP TIMES | DATE |
|---|---|---|---|---|
|  |  |  |  |  |
|  |  |  |  |  |
|  |  |  |  |  |
|  |  |  |  |  |
|  |  |  |  |  |
|  |  |  |  |  |
|  |  |  |  |  |
|  |  |  |  |  |
|  |  |  |  |  |
|  |  |  |  |  |
|  |  |  |  |  |

# SYMPTOM TRACKER

| DATE | TIME | DURATION | DESCRIPTION |
|------|------|----------|-------------|
|      |      |          |             |
|      |      |          |             |
|      |      |          |             |
|      |      |          |             |
|      |      |          |             |
|      |      |          |             |
|      |      |          |             |
|      |      |          |             |
|      |      |          |             |
|      |      |          |             |
|      |      |          |             |
|      |      |          |             |
|      |      |          |             |
|      |      |          |             |
|      |      |          |             |
|      |      |          |             |
|      |      |          |             |
|      |      |          |             |
|      |      |          |             |
|      |      |          |             |
|      |      |          |             |
|      |      |          |             |
|      |      |          |             |
|      |      |          |             |
|      |      |          |             |
|      |      |          |             |
|      |      |          |             |
|      |      |          |             |
|      |      |          |             |
|      |      |          |             |
|      |      |          |             |
| DATE | TIME | DURATION | DESCRIPTION |

# It's okay to ask for help.

# DAILY ENERGY vs MOOD TRACKER

TRACK YOUR DAILY ENERGY AND MOOD USING DIFFERENT COLOURS ON THIS LINE CHART - NOTE YOUR TRIGGERS BELOW.

100

75

50

25

0

ENERGY

| MONDAY | TUESDAY | WEDNESDAY | THURSDAY | FRIDAY | SATURDAY | SUNDAY |
|--------|---------|-----------|----------|--------|----------|--------|

MOOD

# DEREALIZATION DEPERSONALIZATION DISORDER MENTAL HEALTH AND SYMPTOM CHECK LIST
PUT TIME STAMP, Y/N OR 0-5 FOR SEVERITY

| | FREQ. / SEVERITY Y/N | MON | TUES | WED | THURS | FRI | SAT | SUN |
|---|---|---|---|---|---|---|---|---|
| OVERALL MOOD | 0-5 | | | | | | | |
| ENERGY LEVELS | 0-5 | | | | | | | |
| ANXIETY | 0-5 | | | | | | | |
| AMNESIA / MEMORY PROBLEMS | 0-5 | | | | | | | |
| FEELING DETACHED FROM THOUGHTS | Y/N | | | | | | | |
| FEELING DETACHED/ OUTSIDE FROM BODY | Y/N | | | | | | | |
| THINGS FEELING "UNREAL" OR "DREAM LIKE" | Y/N | | | | | | | |
| DEPRESSION | Y/N | | | | | | | |
| EMOTIONAL NUMBNESS | Y/N | | | | | | | |
| RAPID CYCLING MOOD SWINGS | Y/N | | | | | | | |
| FEELING OVERWHELMED | 0-5 | | | | | | | |
| EXPERIENCED FLASHBACKS | Y/N | | | | | | | |
| SENSORY CHANGES E.G. TASTE, SMELL | Y/N | | | | | | | |
| LACK OF MOTIVATION | 0-5 | | | | | | | |
| ATTENDED THERAPY | Y/N | | | | | | | |
| TROUBLE SLEEPING | 0-5 | | | | | | | |
| SELF-CARE ACTIVITIES | Y/N | | | | | | | |
| LOGGED DIARY | Y/N | | | | | | | |
| VISUALS: OBJECTS FURTHER AWAY OR CLOSER | 0-5 | | | | | | | |
| VISUALS: VIVID COLOURS OR BRIGHTNESS | Y/N | | | | | | | |
| AUDIO PERCEPTION PROBLEMS E.G. ALTERED VOICE | 0-5 | | | | | | | |
| ENGAGED IN SOCIAL ACTIVITIES | Y/N | | | | | | | |
| SELF ESTEEM | 0-5 | | | | | | | |
| USED COPING SKILLS | Y/N | | | | | | | |

USE THIS CHART TO TRACK DAILY MOODS, SYMPTOMS AND HABITS. KEEP AN EYE IF THINGS CHANGE AND HOW YOU FEEL AFTER MAKING POSITIVE STEPS.

# DEREALIZATION DEPERSONALIZATION DISORDER MENTAL HEALTH AND SYMPTOM CHECK LIST
## PUT TIME STAMP, Y/N OR 0-5 FOR SEVERITY

| | FREQ. / SEVERITY Y/N | MON | TUES | WED | THURS | FRI | SAT | SUN |
|---|---|---|---|---|---|---|---|---|
| RELATIONSHIP PROBLEMS | Y/N | | | | | | | |
| OVERSLEEPING | 0-5 | | | | | | | |
| FEELING ON AUTOPILOT OR ROBOT | 0-5 | | | | | | | |
| GOING BLANK | 0-5 | | | | | | | |
| PANIC ATTACKS | Y/N | | | | | | | |
| FEELING FEARFUL | Y/N | | | | | | | |
| FEELING AS IF YOU ARE NOT REAL | Y/N | | | | | | | |
| FEELING TIME SLOWED DOWN OR SPED UP | Y/N | | | | | | | |
| FEELING PARALYSIS UNABLE TO MOVE | Y/N | | | | | | | |
| PEOPLE SEEM UNFAMILIAR | Y/N | | | | | | | |
| ENVIRONMENTS SEEM UNFAMILIAR | 0-5 | | | | | | | |
| OBSERVING INTERNAL SENSATIONS | Y/N | | | | | | | |
| FEELING FOGGY | Y/N | | | | | | | |
| OVERTHINKING | 0-5 | | | | | | | |
| CONFUSION | Y/N | | | | | | | |
| DISORGANISATION | 0-5 | | | | | | | |
| DIFFICULTY CONCENTRATING | Y/N | | | | | | | |
| DIFFICULTY COMPLETING TASKS | Y/N | | | | | | | |
| FEELING IRRITABLE | 0-5 | | | | | | | |
| EXPERIENCED RELATIONSHIP PROBLEMS | Y/N | | | | | | | |
| FEELING DETACHED | 0-5 | | | | | | | |
| DECREASED SENSATIONS | Y/N | | | | | | | |
| CONSUMED ALCOHOL | 0-5 | | | | | | | |
| CONSUMED RECREATIONAL DRUGS | Y/N | | | | | | | |

USE THIS CHART TO TRACK DAILY MOODS, SYMPTOMS AND HABITS. KEEP AN EYE IF THINGS CHANGE AND HOW YOU FEEL AFTER MAKING POSITIVE STEPS.

| | FREQ. / SEVERITY Y/N | MON | TUES | WED | THURS | FRI | SAT | SUN |
|---|---|---|---|---|---|---|---|---|
| EXERCISE | MINS | | | | | | | |
| FEELING CALM | 0-5 | | | | | | | |
| FEELING HAPPY | 0-5 | | | | | | | |
| FEELING PRODUCTIVE | 0-5 | | | | | | | |
| WORK/SCHOOL STRESS | 0-5 | | | | | | | |
| GENERAL STRESS | 0-5 | | | | | | | |
| SPOKE TO SOMEONE ABOUT FEELINGS | Y/N | | | | | | | |
| MEDICATION | DOSE | | | | | | | |
| MEDICATION | DOSE | | | | | | | |
| MEDICATION | DOSE | | | | | | | |
| MEDICATION | DOSE | | | | | | | |
| MEDICATION | DOSE | | | | | | | |

FILL IN THE CHARTS TO TRACK EVENTS, MOODS, TRIGGERS, THINGS YOU WANT TO CHANGE, DETAILED NOTES

_____
_____
_____
_____
_____
_____
_____
_____
_____
_____
_____
_____
_____
_____

HOW OFTEN WAS THIS CHART FILLED OUT?
NOT AT ALL    [ ]        1-3X PER WEEK    [ ]        ALMOST EVERY DAY    [ ]        EVERYDAY    [ ]

# TIME OF DAY SYMPTOM TRACKER

TRACK THE SEVERITY OF YOUR SYMPTOMS THROUGHOUT THE DAY USING THE SCALE, USE THE NOTE SECTION BELOW TO LIST THE SYMPTOMS YOU EXPERIENCED. USE THIS TO SEE IF CERTAIN TIMES OF DAY E.G. MEAL TIMES OR FIRST THING IN THE MORNING, ARE TRIGGERS FOR YOU.

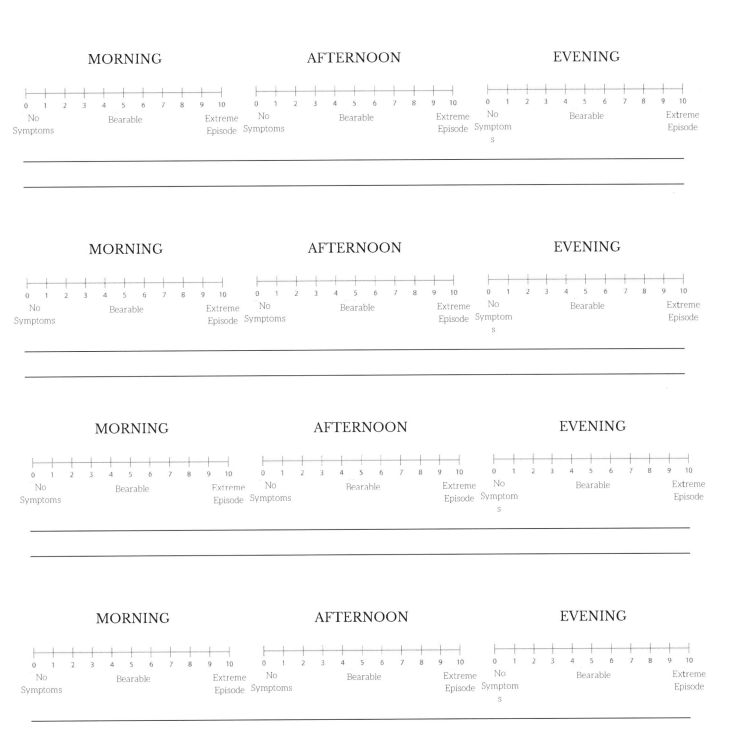

# GROUNDING TECHNIQUES

**WHAT CAN YOU SEE AROUND YOU? WHO OR WHAT SEEMS FAMILIAR? OR DESCRIBE A CALMING PLACE AND WHAT IT LOOKS LIKE.**

_____

_____

_____

_____

_____

**TRY LISTENING TO THE SOUNDS AROUND YOU OR GO SOMEWHERE WITH FAMILIAR CALMING SOUNDS E.G. SOUNDS OF NATURE OR A FAVOURITE SONG. DESCRIBE THOSE SOUNDS.**

_____

_____

_____

_____

_____

**USING ALL YOUR SENSES LIKE SMELL, TASTE, TOUCH, HEARING, DESCRIBE YOUR SURROUNDINGS OR YOUR FAVOURITE EXPERIENCES E.G. FAVOURITE FOOD.**

_____

_____

_____

_____

_____

**HOW DO YOU CURRENTLY FEEL? AND WHAT DO YOU THINK ABOUT HOW YOU CURRENTLY FEEL? CAN YOU CHALLENGE THOSE THOUGHTS?**

_____

_____

_____

_____

_____

**WHAT IS YOUR PREFERRED GROUNDING TECHNIQUE? E.G. BREATHING SLOWLY? DISTRACTING YOURSELF? MAKE A LIST OF TECHNIQUES YOU CAN USE WHEN YOU FEEL YOUR SYMPTOMS ARE BAD OR YOUR ANXIETY OR MOOD AROUND THEM ARE TROUBLING YOU.**

_____

_____

_____

_____

_____

# PRACTICAL STRATEGIES FOR DISOCCIATION

TRIGGER WARNING:
WHAT MAY HELP ONE PERSON MAY TRIGGER OTHERS, USE THESE TECHNIQUES WITH CAUTION AND MODIFY THEM AROUND YOU.

### WHAT SITUATIONS DO YOU FIND TRIGGERING OR EXACERBATE YOUR DEPERSONALIZATION/DEREALIZATION?

_____
_____
_____
_____
_____

### WHAT FEATURES DO THESE SCENARIOS SHARE? ARE THEY STRESSFUL? UPSETTING? RANDOM? INVOLVE FAMILY? PAST TRAUMA?

_____
_____
_____
_____
_____

### HOW DO YOU FEEL DURING THESE EVENTS? WHAT ARE YOU SYMPTOMS AND EMOTIONS, AND WHAT ARE YOUR THOUGHTS ON THEM?

_____
_____
_____
_____
_____

### HOW CAN YOU PREPARE FOR THESE SITUATIONS IN THE FUTURE?

_____
_____
_____
_____
_____

### WHAT CHANGES CAN I MAKE TO IMPROVE MY SYMPTOMS AND FEELINGS DURING (OR AFTER) THESE SYMPTOMS? (E.G. GROUNDING TECHNIQUES, CHANGING THOUGHT PATTERNS, CALMING RITUALS TO LOWER STRESS LEVELS DURING SOCIAL SITUATIONS ETC)

_____
_____
_____
_____
_____

# TIME OF DAY ANXIETY & MOOD TRACKER

TRACK YOUR ANXIETY FLUCTUATIONS THROUGHOUT THE DAY TO SPOT POSSIBLE TRIGGERS AND PATTERNS TO MANAGE YOUR STRESS/ANXIETY LEVELS MORE EFFECTIVELY. WRITE TRIGGERS AND COPING MECHANISMS IN THE NOTES.

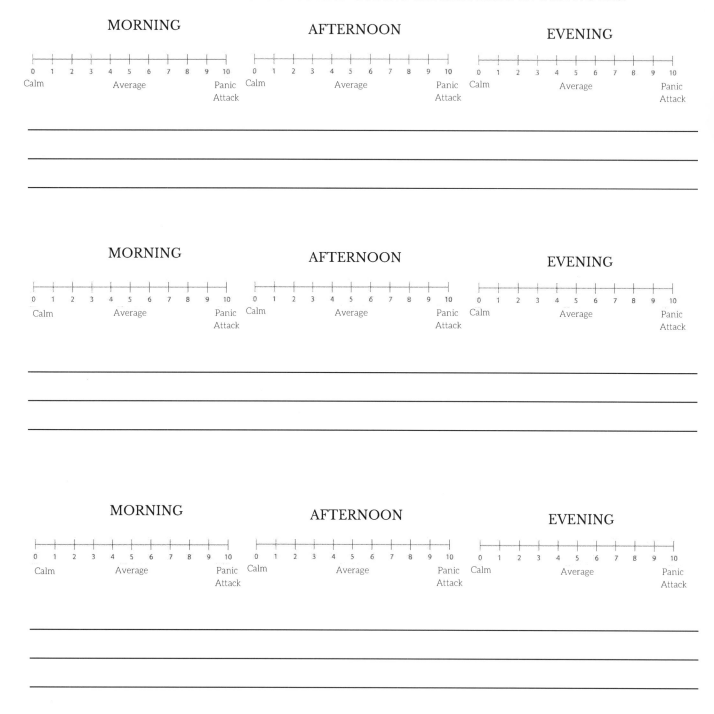

# GENERALIZED ANXIETY OVERVIEW WORKSHEET

WHAT SITUATIONS MAKE ME FEEL ANXIOUS?

_____
_____
_____
_____

WHAT THOUGHTS DO I HAVE DURING EPISODES OF ANXIETY?
(TAKE A NOTE OF NEGATIVE THOUGHTS ABOUT YOURSELF AND YOUR ABILITY TO HANDLE THE SITUATION)

_____
_____
_____

IS THERE ANYTHING FLAWED IN MY THINKING DURING THESE EPISODES?

_____
_____
_____
_____

WHAT IS THE REALITY OF THE SITUATION AND WHAT CAN I THINK INSTEAD?

_____
_____
_____

WHAT CHANGES CAN I MAKE TO IMPROVE MY ANXIETY DURING THIS SITUATION?
(E.G. CHANGING THOUGHT PATTERNS, CALMING RITUALS TO LOWER STRESS LEVELS
DURING SITUATIONS ETC)

_____
_____
_____

# SLEEP TRACKER

| TOTAL SLEEP TIME | SLEEP START TIME | WAKE UP TIME | NAP TIMES | DATE |
|---|---|---|---|---|
| | | | | |
| | | | | |
| | | | | |
| | | | | |
| | | | | |
| | | | | |
| | | | | |
| | | | | |
| | | | | |
| | | | | |
| | | | | |
| | | | | |

# SYMPTOM TRACKER

| DATE | TIME | DURATION | DESCRIPTION |
|------|------|----------|-------------|
|      |      |          |             |
|      |      |          |             |
|      |      |          |             |
|      |      |          |             |
|      |      |          |             |
|      |      |          |             |
|      |      |          |             |
|      |      |          |             |
|      |      |          |             |
|      |      |          |             |
|      |      |          |             |
|      |      |          |             |
|      |      |          |             |
|      |      |          |             |
|      |      |          |             |
|      |      |          |             |
|      |      |          |             |
|      |      |          |             |
|      |      |          |             |
|      |      |          |             |
|      |      |          |             |
|      |      |          |             |
|      |      |          |             |
|      |      |          |             |
|      |      |          |             |
|      |      |          |             |
|      |      |          |             |
|      |      |          |             |
|      |      |          |             |
|      |      |          |             |
|      |      |          |             |
|      |      |          |             |
|      |      |          |             |

# DAILY ENERGY vs MOOD TRACKER

TRACK YOUR DAILY ENERGY AND MOOD USING DIFFERENT COLOURS ON THIS LINE CHART - NOTE YOUR TRIGGERS BELOW.

100

75

50

25

0

ENERGY

| MONDAY | TUESDAY | WEDNESDAY | THURSDAY | FRIDAY | SATURDAY | SUNDAY |
|--------|---------|-----------|----------|--------|----------|--------|

MOOD

# DEREALIZATION DEPERSONALIZATION DISORDER MENTAL HEALTH AND SYMPTOM CHECK LIST
PUT TIME STAMP, Y/N OR 0-5 FOR SEVERITY

| | FREQ. / SEVERITY Y/N | MON | TUES | WED | THURS | FRI | SAT | SUN |
|---|---|---|---|---|---|---|---|---|
| OVERALL MOOD | 0-5 | | | | | | | |
| ENERGY LEVELS | 0-5 | | | | | | | |
| ANXIETY | 0-5 | | | | | | | |
| AMNESIA / MEMORY PROBLEMS | 0-5 | | | | | | | |
| FEELING DETACHED FROM THOUGHTS | Y/N | | | | | | | |
| FEELING DETACHED/ OUTSIDE FROM BODY | Y/N | | | | | | | |
| THINGS FEELING "UNREAL" OR "DREAM LIKE" | Y/N | | | | | | | |
| DEPRESSION | Y/N | | | | | | | |
| EMOTIONAL NUMBNESS | Y/N | | | | | | | |
| RAPID CYCLING MOOD SWINGS | Y/N | | | | | | | |
| FEELING OVERWHELMED | 0-5 | | | | | | | |
| EXPERIENCED FLASHBACKS | Y/N | | | | | | | |
| SENSORY CHANGES E.G. TASTE, SMELL | Y/N | | | | | | | |
| LACK OF MOTIVATION | 0-5 | | | | | | | |
| ATTENDED THERAPY | Y/N | | | | | | | |
| TROUBLE SLEEPING | 0-5 | | | | | | | |
| SELF-CARE ACTIVITIES | Y/N | | | | | | | |
| LOGGED DIARY | Y/N | | | | | | | |
| VISUALS: OBJECTS FURTHER AWAY OR CLOSER | 0-5 | | | | | | | |
| VISUALS: VIVID COLOURS OR BRIGHTNESS | Y/N | | | | | | | |
| AUDIO PERCEPTION PROBLEMS E.G. ALTERED VOICE | 0-5 | | | | | | | |
| ENGAGED IN SOCIAL ACTIVITIES | Y/N | | | | | | | |
| SELF ESTEEM | 0-5 | | | | | | | |
| USED COPING SKILLS | Y/N | | | | | | | |

USE THIS CHART TO TRACK DAILY MOODS, SYMPTOMS AND HABITS. KEEP AN EYE IF THINGS CHANGE AND HOW YOU FEEL AFTER MAKING POSITIVE STEPS.

# DEREALIZATION DEPERSONALIZATION DISORDER MENTAL HEALTH AND SYMPTOM CHECK LIST
## PUT TIME STAMP, Y/N OR 0-5 FOR SEVERITY

| | FREQ. / SEVERITY Y/N | MON | TUES | WED | THURS | FRI | SAT | SUN |
|---|---|---|---|---|---|---|---|---|
| RELATIONSHIP PROBLEMS | Y/N | | | | | | | |
| OVERSLEEPING | 0-5 | | | | | | | |
| FEELING ON AUTOPILOT OR ROBOT | 0-5 | | | | | | | |
| GOING BLANK | 0-5 | | | | | | | |
| PANIC ATTACKS | Y/N | | | | | | | |
| FEELING FEARFUL | Y/N | | | | | | | |
| FEELING AS IF YOU ARE NOT REAL | Y/N | | | | | | | |
| FEELING TIME SLOWED DOWN OR SPED UP | Y/N | | | | | | | |
| FEELING PARALYSIS UNABLE TO MOVE | Y/N | | | | | | | |
| PEOPLE SEEM UNFAMILIAR | Y/N | | | | | | | |
| ENVIRONMENTS SEEM UNFAMILIAR | 0-5 | | | | | | | |
| OBSERVING INTERNAL SENSATIONS | Y/N | | | | | | | |
| FEELING FOGGY | Y/N | | | | | | | |
| OVERTHINKING | 0-5 | | | | | | | |
| CONFUSION | Y/N | | | | | | | |
| DISORGANISATION | 0-5 | | | | | | | |
| DIFFICULTY CONCENTRATING | Y/N | | | | | | | |
| DIFFICULTY COMPLETING TASKS | Y/N | | | | | | | |
| FEELING IRRITABLE | 0-5 | | | | | | | |
| EXPERIENCED RELATIONSHIP PROBLEMS | Y/N | | | | | | | |
| FEELING DETACHED | 0-5 | | | | | | | |
| DECREASED SENSATIONS | Y/N | | | | | | | |
| CONSUMED ALCOHOL | 0-5 | | | | | | | |
| CONSUMED RECREATIONAL DRUGS | Y/N | | | | | | | |

USE THIS CHART TO TRACK DAILY MOODS, SYMPTOMS AND HABITS. KEEP AN EYE IF THINGS CHANGE AND HOW YOU FEEL AFTER MAKING POSITIVE STEPS.

| | FREQ. / SEVERITY Y/N | MON | TUES | WED | THURS | FRI | SAT | SUN |
|---|---|---|---|---|---|---|---|---|
| EXERCISE | MINS | | | | | | | |
| FEELING CALM | 0-5 | | | | | | | |
| FEELING HAPPY | 0-5 | | | | | | | |
| FEELING PRODUCTIVE | 0-5 | | | | | | | |
| WORK/SCHOOL STRESS | 0-5 | | | | | | | |
| GENERAL STRESS | 0-5 | | | | | | | |
| SPOKE TO SOMEONE ABOUT FEELINGS | Y/N | | | | | | | |
| MEDICATION | DOSE | | | | | | | |
| MEDICATION | DOSE | | | | | | | |
| MEDICATION | DOSE | | | | | | | |
| MEDICATION | DOSE | | | | | | | |
| MEDICATION | DOSE | | | | | | | |

FILL IN THE CHARTS TO TRACK EVENTS, MOODS, TRIGGERS, THINGS YOU WANT TO CHANGE, DETAILED NOTES

_____
_____
_____
_____
_____
_____
_____
_____
_____
_____
_____
_____
_____

HOW OFTEN WAS THIS CHART FILLED OUT?
NOT AT ALL   [ ]        1-3X PER WEEK   [ ]        ALMOST EVERY DAY   [ ]        EVERYDAY   [ ]

# TIME OF DAY SYMPTOM TRACKER

TRACK THE SEVERITY OF YOUR SYMPTOMS THROUGHOUT THE DAY USING THE SCALE, USE THE NOTE SECTION BELOW TO LIST THE SYMPTOMS YOU EXPERIENCED. USE THIS TO SEE IF CERTAIN TIMES OF DAY E.G. MEAL TIMES OR FIRST THING IN THE MORNING, ARE TRIGGERS FOR YOU.

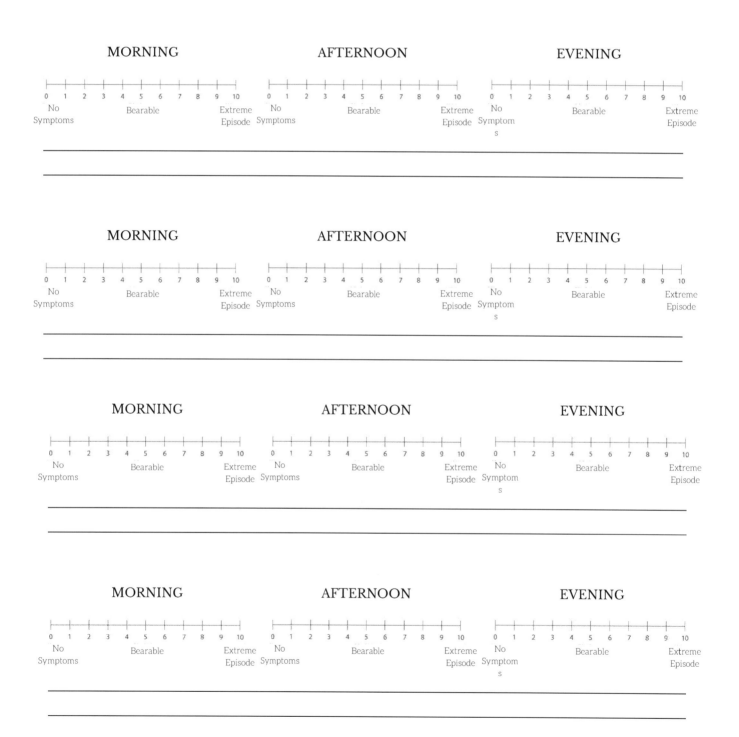

# GROUNDING TECHNIQUES

**WHAT CAN YOU SEE AROUND YOU? WHO OR WHAT SEEMS FAMILIAR? OR DESCRIBE A CALMING PLACE AND WHAT IT LOOKS LIKE.**

**TRY LISTENING TO THE SOUNDS AROUND YOU OR GO SOMEWHERE WITH FAMILIAR CALMING SOUNDS E.G. SOUNDS OF NATURE OR A FAVOURITE SONG. DESCRIBE THOSE SOUNDS.**

**USING ALL YOUR SENSES LIKE SMELL, TASTE, TOUCH, HEARING, DESCRIBE YOUR SURROUNDINGS OR YOUR FAVOURITE EXPERIENCES E.G. FAVOURITE FOOD.**

**HOW DO YOU CURRENTLY FEEL? AND WHAT DO YOU THINK ABOUT HOW YOU CURRENTLY FEEL? CAN YOU CHALLENGE THOSE THOUGHTS?**

**WHAT IS YOUR PREFERRED GROUNDING TECHNIQUE? E.G. BREATHING SLOWLY? DISTRACTING YOURSELF? MAKE A LIST OF TECHNIQUES YOU CAN USE WHEN YOU FEEL YOUR SYMPTOMS ARE BAD OR YOUR ANXIETY OR MOOD AROUND THEM ARE TROUBLING YOU.**

# PRACTICAL STRATEGIES FOR DISOCCIATION

TRIGGER WARNING:
WHAT MAY HELP ONE PERSON MAY TRIGGER OTHERS, USE THESE TECHNIQUES WITH CAUTION AND MODIFY THEM AROUND YOU.

**WHAT SITUATIONS DO YOU FIND TRIGGERING OR EXACERBATE YOUR DEPERSONALIZATION/DEREALIZATION?**

_____
_____
_____
_____
_____

**WHAT FEATURES DO THESE SCENARIOS SHARE? ARE THEY STRESSFUL? UPSETTING? RANDOM? INVOLVE FAMILY? PAST TRAUMA?**

_____
_____
_____
_____
_____

**HOW DO YOU FEEL DURING THESE EVENTS? WHAT ARE YOU SYMPTOMS AND EMOTIONS, AND WHAT ARE YOUR THOUGHTS ON THEM?**

_____
_____
_____
_____
_____

**HOW CAN YOU PREPARE FOR THESE SITUATIONS IN THE FUTURE?**

_____
_____
_____
_____
_____

**WHAT CHANGES CAN I MAKE TO IMPROVE MY SYMPTOMS AND FEELINGS DURING (OR AFTER) THESE SYMPTOMS? (E.G. GROUNDING TECHNIQUES, CHANGING THOUGHT PATTERNS, CALMING RITUALS TO LOWER STRESS LEVELS DURING SOCIAL SITUATIONS ETC)**

_____
_____
_____
_____
_____

# TIME OF DAY ANXIETY & MOOD TRACKER

TRACK YOUR ANXIETY FLUCTUATIONS THROUGHOUT THE DAY TO SPOT POSSIBLE
TRIGGERS AND PATTERNS TO MANAGE YOUR STRESS/ANXIETY LEVELS MORE
EFFECTIVELY. WRITE TRIGGERS AND COPING MECHANISMS IN THE NOTES.

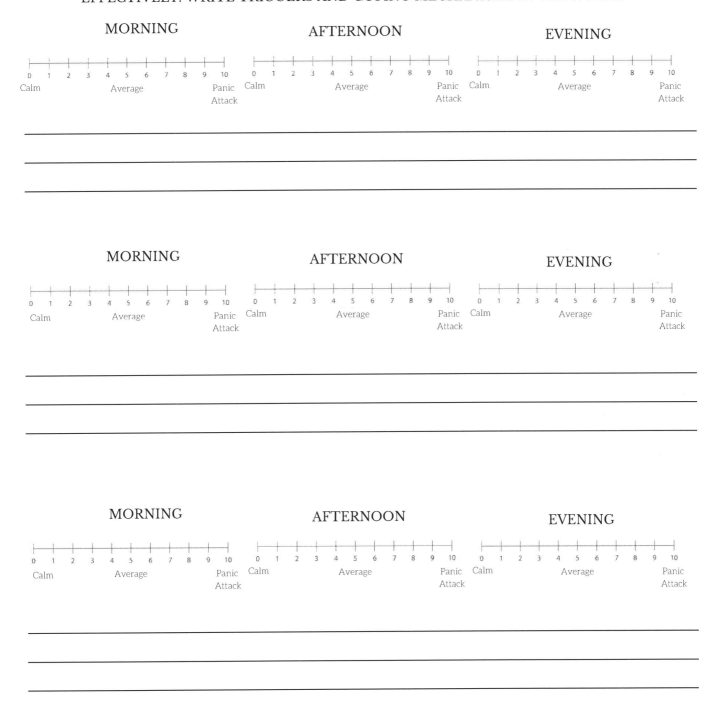

# GENERALIZED ANXIETY OVERVIEW WORKSHEET

WHAT SITUATIONS MAKE ME FEEL ANXIOUS?

_____
_____
_____
_____
_____

WHAT THOUGHTS DO I HAVE DURING EPISODES OF ANXIETY?
(TAKE A NOTE OF NEGATIVE THOUGHTS ABOUT YOURSELF AND YOUR ABILITY TO HANDLE THE SITUATION)

_____
_____
_____
_____

IS THERE ANYTHING FLAWED IN MY THINKING DURING THESE EPISODES?

_____
_____
_____
_____
_____

WHAT IS THE REALITY OF THE SITUATION AND WHAT CAN I THINK INSTEAD?

_____
_____
_____
_____

WHAT CHANGES CAN I MAKE TO IMPROVE MY ANXIETY DURING THIS SITUATION?
(E.G. CHANGING THOUGHT PATTERNS, CALMING RITUALS TO LOWER STRESS LEVELS DURING SITUATIONS ETC)

_____
_____
_____
_____

# SLEEP TRACKER

| TOTAL SLEEP TIME | SLEEP START TIME | WAKE UP TIME | NAP TIMES | DATE |
|---|---|---|---|---|
|  |  |  |  |  |
|  |  |  |  |  |
|  |  |  |  |  |
|  |  |  |  |  |
|  |  |  |  |  |
|  |  |  |  |  |
|  |  |  |  |  |
|  |  |  |  |  |
|  |  |  |  |  |
|  |  |  |  |  |
|  |  |  |  |  |
|  |  |  |  |  |

# SYMPTOM TRACKER

| DATE | TIME | DURATION | DESCRIPTION |
|------|------|----------|-------------|
|      |      |          |             |
|      |      |          |             |
|      |      |          |             |
|      |      |          |             |
|      |      |          |             |
|      |      |          |             |
|      |      |          |             |
|      |      |          |             |
|      |      |          |             |
|      |      |          |             |
|      |      |          |             |
|      |      |          |             |
|      |      |          |             |
|      |      |          |             |
|      |      |          |             |
|      |      |          |             |
|      |      |          |             |
|      |      |          |             |
|      |      |          |             |
|      |      |          |             |
|      |      |          |             |
|      |      |          |             |
|      |      |          |             |
|      |      |          |             |
|      |      |          |             |
|      |      |          |             |
|      |      |          |             |
|      |      |          |             |
|      |      |          |             |
|      |      |          |             |
|      |      |          |             |
|      |      |          |             |

Give yourself credit for how far you
have come.
Be kind to yourself.
It is okay to rest.

# *WHAT MOMENT ARE YOU MOST GRATEFUL FOR?*

ANSWER THESE QUESTIONS TO BREAK OUT OF NEGATIVE
THOUGHT PATTERNS AND REFOCUS ON THE THINGS THAT MAKE
YOU HAPPY AND GRATEFUL.

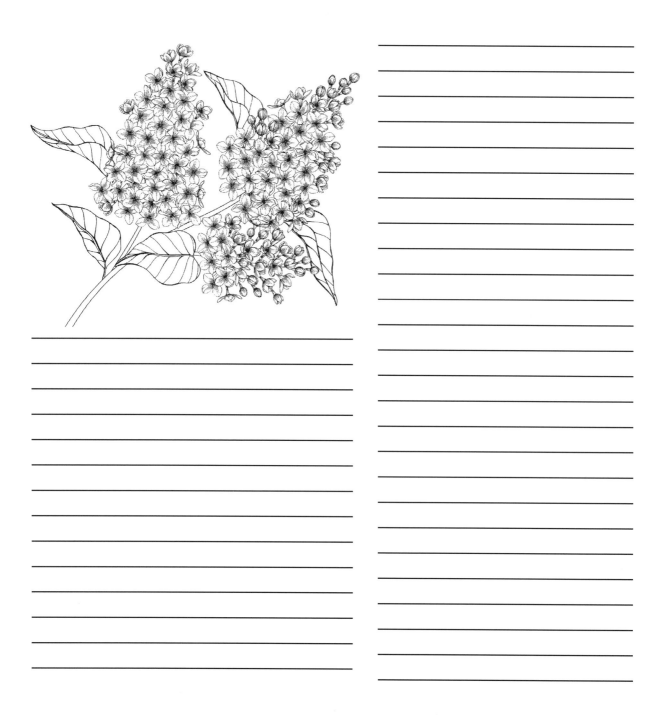

# DAILY ENERGY vs MOOD TRACKER

TRACK YOUR DAILY ENERGY AND MOOD USING DIFFERENT COLOURS ON THIS LINE CHART - NOTE YOUR TRIGGERS BELOW.

100

75

50

25

0

ENERGY

| MONDAY | TUESDAY | WEDNESDAY | THURSDAY | FRIDAY | SATURDAY | SUNDAY |
|--------|---------|-----------|----------|--------|----------|--------|

MOOD

# DEREALIZATION DEPERSONALIZATION DISORDER MENTAL HEALTH AND SYMPTOM CHECK LIST
PUT TIME STAMP, Y/N OR 0-5 FOR SEVERITY

| | FREQ. / SEVERITY Y/N | MON | TUES | WED | THURS | FRI | SAT | SUN |
|---|---|---|---|---|---|---|---|---|
| OVERALL MOOD | 0-5 | | | | | | | |
| ENERGY LEVELS | 0-5 | | | | | | | |
| ANXIETY | 0-5 | | | | | | | |
| AMNESIA / MEMORY PROBLEMS | 0-5 | | | | | | | |
| FEELING DETACHED FROM THOUGHTS | Y/N | | | | | | | |
| FEELING DETACHED/ OUTSIDE FROM BODY | Y/N | | | | | | | |
| THINGS FEELING "UNREAL" OR "DREAM LIKE" | Y/N | | | | | | | |
| DEPRESSION | Y/N | | | | | | | |
| EMOTIONAL NUMBNESS | Y/N | | | | | | | |
| RAPID CYCLING MOOD SWINGS | Y/N | | | | | | | |
| FEELING OVERWHELMED | 0-5 | | | | | | | |
| EXPERIENCED FLASHBACKS | Y/N | | | | | | | |
| SENSORY CHANGES E.G. TASTE, SMELL | Y/N | | | | | | | |
| LACK OF MOTIVATION | 0-5 | | | | | | | |
| ATTENDED THERAPY | Y/N | | | | | | | |
| TROUBLE SLEEPING | 0-5 | | | | | | | |
| SELF-CARE ACTIVITIES | Y/N | | | | | | | |
| LOGGED DIARY | Y/N | | | | | | | |
| VISUALS: OBJECTS FURTHER AWAY OR CLOSER | 0-5 | | | | | | | |
| VISUALS: VIVID COLOURS OR BRIGHTNESS | Y/N | | | | | | | |
| AUDIO PERCEPTION PROBLEMS E.G. ALTERED VOICE | 0-5 | | | | | | | |
| ENGAGED IN SOCIAL ACTIVITIES | Y/N | | | | | | | |
| SELF ESTEEM | 0-5 | | | | | | | |
| USED COPING SKILLS | Y/N | | | | | | | |

USE THIS CHART TO TRACK DAILY MOODS, SYMPTOMS AND HABITS. KEEP AN EYE IF THINGS CHANGE AND HOW YOU FEEL AFTER MAKING POSITIVE STEPS.

# DEREALIZATION DEPERSONALIZATION DISORDER MENTAL HEALTH AND SYMPTOM CHECK LIST
## PUT TIME STAMP,Y/N OR 0-5 FOR SEVERITY

| | FREQ. / SEVERITY Y/N | MON | TUES | WED | THURS | FRI | SAT | SUN |
|---|---|---|---|---|---|---|---|---|
| RELATIONSHIP PROBLEMS | Y/N | | | | | | | |
| OVERSLEEPING | 0-5 | | | | | | | |
| FEELING ON AUTOPILOT OR ROBOT | 0-5 | | | | | | | |
| GOING BLANK | 0-5 | | | | | | | |
| PANIC ATTACKS | Y/N | | | | | | | |
| FEELING FEARFUL | Y/N | | | | | | | |
| FEELING AS IF YOU ARE NOT REAL | Y/N | | | | | | | |
| FEELING TIME SLOWED DOWN OR SPED UP | Y/N | | | | | | | |
| FEELING PARALYSIS UNABLE TO MOVE | Y/N | | | | | | | |
| PEOPLE SEEM UNFAMILIAR | Y/N | | | | | | | |
| ENVIRONMENTS SEEM UNFAMILIAR | 0-5 | | | | | | | |
| OBSERVING INTERNAL SENSATIONS | Y/N | | | | | | | |
| FEELING FOGGY | Y/N | | | | | | | |
| OVERTHINKING | 0-5 | | | | | | | |
| CONFUSION | Y/N | | | | | | | |
| DISORGANISATION | 0-5 | | | | | | | |
| DIFFICULTY CONCENTRATING | Y/N | | | | | | | |
| DIFFICULTY COMPLETING TASKS | Y/N | | | | | | | |
| FEELING IRRITABLE | 0-5 | | | | | | | |
| EXPERIENCED RELATIONSHIP PROBLEMS | Y/N | | | | | | | |
| FEELING DETACHED | 0-5 | | | | | | | |
| DECREASED SENSATIONS | Y/N | | | | | | | |
| CONSUMED ALCOHOL | 0-5 | | | | | | | |
| CONSUMED RECREATIONAL DRUGS | Y/N | | | | | | | |

USE THIS CHART TO TRACK DAILY MOODS, SYMPTOMS AND HABITS. KEEP AN EYE IF THINGS CHANGE AND HOW YOU FEEL AFTER MAKING POSITIVE STEPS.

| | FREQ. / SEVERITY Y/N | MON | TUES | WED | THURS | FRI | SAT | SUN |
|---|---|---|---|---|---|---|---|---|
| EXERCISE | MINS | | | | | | | |
| FEELING CALM | 0-5 | | | | | | | |
| FEELING HAPPY | 0-5 | | | | | | | |
| FEELING PRODUCTIVE | 0-5 | | | | | | | |
| WORK/SCHOOL STRESS | 0-5 | | | | | | | |
| GENERAL STRESS | 0-5 | | | | | | | |
| SPOKE TO SOMEONE ABOUT FEELINGS | Y/N | | | | | | | |
| MEDICATION | DOSE | | | | | | | |
| MEDICATION | DOSE | | | | | | | |
| MEDICATION | DOSE | | | | | | | |
| MEDICATION | DOSE | | | | | | | |
| MEDICATION | DOSE | | | | | | | |

FILL IN THE CHARTS TO TRACK EVENTS, MOODS, TRIGGERS, THINGS YOU WANT TO CHANGE, DETAILED NOTES

_____
_____
_____
_____
_____
_____
_____
_____
_____
_____
_____
_____
_____

HOW OFTEN WAS THIS CHART FILLED OUT?
NOT AT ALL     [ ]          1-3X PER WEEK     [ ]          ALMOST EVERY DAY     [ ]          EVERYDAY     [ ]

# TIME OF DAY SYMPTOM TRACKER

TRACK THE SEVERITY OF YOUR SYMPTOMS THROUGHOUT THE DAY USING THE
SCALE, USE THE NOTE SECTION BELOW TO LIST THE SYMPTOMS YOU EXPERIENCED.
USE THIS TO SEE IF CERTAIN TIMES OF DAY E.G. MEAL TIMES OR FIRST THING IN THE
MORNING, ARE TRIGGERS FOR YOU.

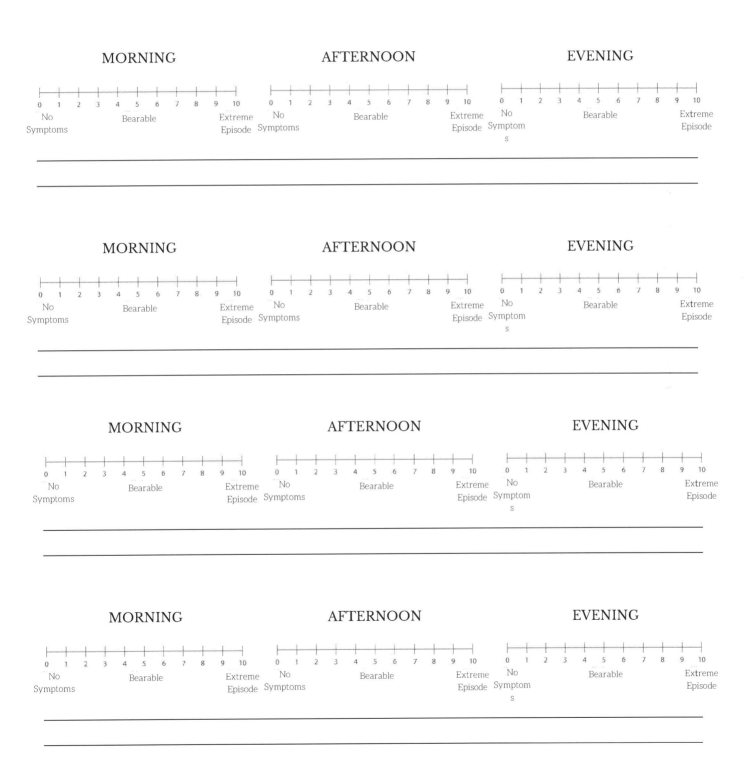

# GROUNDING TECHNIQUES

**WHAT CAN YOU SEE AROUND YOU? WHO OR WHAT SEEMS FAMILIAR? OR DESCRIBE A CALMING PLACE AND WHAT IT LOOKS LIKE.**

_____

_____

_____

_____

**TRY LISTENING TO THE SOUNDS AROUND YOU OR GO SOMEWHERE WITH FAMILIAR CALMING SOUNDS E.G. SOUNDS OF NATURE OR A FAVOURITE SONG. DESCRIBE THOSE SOUNDS.**

_____

_____

_____

_____

**USING ALL YOUR SENSES LIKE SMELL, TASTE, TOUCH, HEARING, DESCRIBE YOUR SURROUNDINGS OR YOUR FAVOURITE EXPERIENCES E.G. FAVOURITE FOOD.**

_____

_____

_____

_____

**HOW DO YOU CURRENTLY FEEL? AND WHAT DO YOU THINK ABOUT HOW YOU CURRENTLY FEEL? CAN YOU CHALLENGE THOSE THOUGHTS?**

_____

_____

_____

**WHAT IS YOUR PREFERRED GROUNDING TECHNIQUE? E.G. BREATHING SLOWLY? DISTRACTING YOURSELF? MAKE A LIST OF TECHNIQUES YOU CAN USE WHEN YOU FEEL YOUR SYMPTOMS ARE BAD OR YOUR ANXIETY OR MOOD AROUND THEM ARE TROUBLING YOU.**

_____

_____

_____

_____

# PRACTICAL STRATEGIES FOR DISOCCIATION

**WHAT SITUATIONS DO YOU FIND TRIGGERING OR EXACERBATE YOUR DEPERSONALIZATION/DEREALIZATION?**

_____

_____

_____

_____

_____

**WHAT FEATURES DO THESE SCENARIOS SHARE? ARE THEY STRESSFUL? UPSETTING? RANDOM? INVOLVE FAMILY? PAST TRAUMA?**

_____

_____

_____

_____

**HOW DO YOU FEEL DURING THESE EVENTS? WHAT ARE YOU SYMPTOMS AND EMOTIONS, AND WHAT ARE YOUR THOUGHTS ON THEM?**

_____

_____

_____

_____

**HOW CAN YOU PREPARE FOR THESE SITUATIONS IN THE FUTURE?**

_____

_____

_____

_____

**WHAT CHANGES CAN I MAKE TO IMPROVE MY SYMPTOMS AND FEELINGS DURING (OR AFTER) THESE SYMPTOMS? (E.G. GROUNDING TECHNIQUES, CHANGING THOUGHT PATTERNS, CALMING RITUALS TO LOWER STRESS LEVELS DURING SOCIAL SITUATIONS ETC)**

_____

_____

_____

_____

# TIME OF DAY ANXIETY & MOOD TRACKER

TRACK YOUR ANXIETY FLUCTUATIONS THROUGHOUT THE DAY TO SPOT POSSIBLE TRIGGERS AND PATTERNS TO MANAGE YOUR STRESS/ANXIETY LEVELS MORE EFFECTIVELY. WRITE TRIGGERS AND COPING MECHANISMS IN THE NOTES.

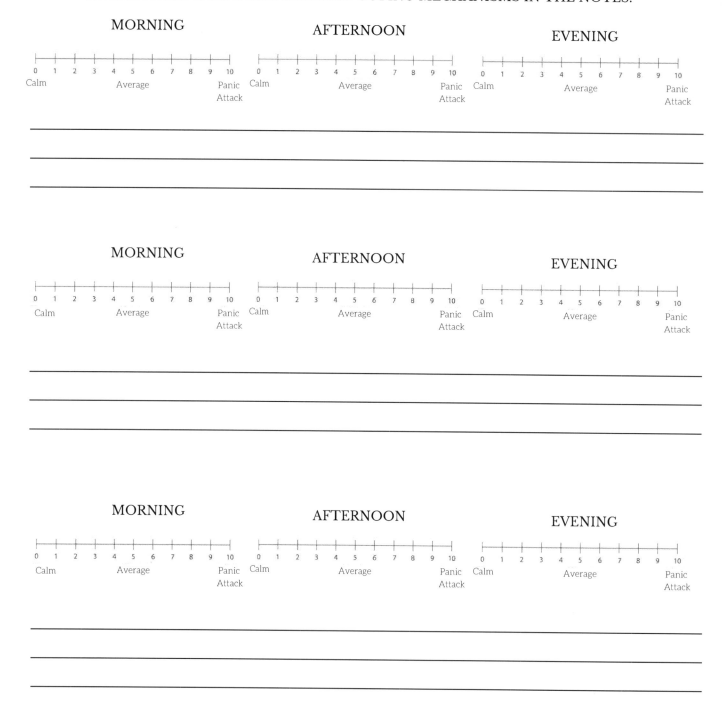

### MORNING

0  1  2  3  4  5  6  7  8  9  10
Calm        Average        Panic Attack

### AFTERNOON

0  1  2  3  4  5  6  7  8  9  10
Calm        Average        Panic Attack

### EVENING

0  1  2  3  4  5  6  7  8  9  10
Calm        Average        Panic Attack

### MORNING

0  1  2  3  4  5  6  7  8  9  10
Calm        Average        Panic Attack

### AFTERNOON

0  1  2  3  4  5  6  7  8  9  10
Calm        Average        Panic Attack

### EVENING

0  1  2  3  4  5  6  7  8  9  10
Calm        Average        Panic Attack

### MORNING

0  1  2  3  4  5  6  7  8  9  10
Calm        Average        Panic Attack

### AFTERNOON

0  1  2  3  4  5  6  7  8  9  10
Calm        Average        Panic Attack

### EVENING

0  1  2  3  4  5  6  7  8  9  10
Calm        Average        Panic Attack

# GENERALIZED ANXIETY OVERVIEW WORKSHEET

WHAT SITUATIONS MAKE ME FEEL ANXIOUS?

_____
_____
_____
_____
_____

WHAT THOUGHTS DO I HAVE DURING EPISODES OF ANXIETY?
(TAKE A NOTE OF NEGATIVE THOUGHTS ABOUT YOURSELF AND YOUR ABILITY TO HANDLE THE SITUATION)

_____
_____
_____
_____

IS THERE ANYTHING FLAWED IN MY THINKING DURING THESE EPISODES?

_____
_____
_____
_____

WHAT IS THE REALITY OF THE SITUATION AND WHAT CAN I THINK INSTEAD?

_____
_____
_____
_____

WHAT CHANGES CAN I MAKE TO IMPROVE MY ANXIETY DURING THIS SITUATION?
(E.G. CHANGING THOUGHT PATTERNS, CALMING RITUALS TO LOWER STRESS LEVELS
DURING SITUATIONS ETC)

_____
_____
_____
_____

# SLEEP TRACKER

| TOTAL SLEEP TIME | SLEEP START TIME | WAKE UP TIME | NAP TIMES | DATE |
|---|---|---|---|---|
| | | | | |
| | | | | |
| | | | | |
| | | | | |
| | | | | |
| | | | | |
| | | | | |
| | | | | |
| | | | | |
| | | | | |
| | | | | |
| | | | | |

# SYMPTOM TRACKER

| DATE | TIME | DURATION | DESCRIPTION |
|------|------|----------|-------------|
|      |      |          |             |
|      |      |          |             |
|      |      |          |             |
|      |      |          |             |
|      |      |          |             |
|      |      |          |             |
|      |      |          |             |
|      |      |          |             |
|      |      |          |             |
|      |      |          |             |
|      |      |          |             |
|      |      |          |             |
|      |      |          |             |
|      |      |          |             |
|      |      |          |             |
|      |      |          |             |
|      |      |          |             |
|      |      |          |             |
|      |      |          |             |
|      |      |          |             |
|      |      |          |             |
|      |      |          |             |
|      |      |          |             |
|      |      |          |             |
|      |      |          |             |
|      |      |          |             |
|      |      |          |             |
|      |      |          |             |
|      |      |          |             |
|      |      |          |             |
|      |      |          |             |
|      |      |          |             |
|      |      |          |             |
|      |      |          |             |

Write down your triggers. Keep working through them. Some people avoid them, some people write out the underlying emotions and negate them with new thought patterns, some need medications, therapy. Whatever you need, do not expect perfection in recovery, just work towards progress.

# WHAT BODY PART ARE YOU GRATEFUL FOR?

ANSWER THESE QUESTIONS TO BREAK OUT OF NEGATIVE
THOUGHT PATTERNS AND REFOCUS ON THE THINGS THAT MAKE
YOU HAPPY AND GRATEFUL.

# DAILY ENERGY vs MOOD TRACKER

TRACK YOUR DAILY ENERGY AND MOOD USING DIFFERENT COLOURS ON THIS LINE CHART - NOTE YOUR TRIGGERS BELOW.

100

75

50

25

0

MONDAY   TUESDAY   WEDNESDAY   THURSDAY   FRIDAY   SATURDAY   SUNDAY

ENERGY

MOOD

# DEREALIZATION DEPERSONALIZATION DISORDER MENTAL HEALTH AND SYMPTOM CHECK LIST
PUT TIME STAMP, Y/N OR 0-5 FOR SEVERITY

| | FREQ. / SEVERITY Y/N | MON | TUES | WED | THURS | FRI | SAT | SUN |
|---|---|---|---|---|---|---|---|---|
| OVERALL MOOD | 0-5 | | | | | | | |
| ENERGY LEVELS | 0-5 | | | | | | | |
| ANXIETY | 0-5 | | | | | | | |
| AMNESIA / MEMORY PROBLEMS | 0-5 | | | | | | | |
| FEELING DETACHED FROM THOUGHTS | Y/N | | | | | | | |
| FEELING DETACHED/ OUTSIDE FROM BODY | Y/N | | | | | | | |
| THINGS FEELING "UNREAL" OR "DREAM LIKE" | Y/N | | | | | | | |
| DEPRESSION | Y/N | | | | | | | |
| EMOTIONAL NUMBNESS | Y/N | | | | | | | |
| RAPID CYCLING MOOD SWINGS | Y/N | | | | | | | |
| FEELING OVERWHELMED | 0-5 | | | | | | | |
| EXPERIENCED FLASHBACKS | Y/N | | | | | | | |
| SENSORY CHANGES E.G. TASTE, SMELL | Y/N | | | | | | | |
| LACK OF MOTIVATION | 0-5 | | | | | | | |
| ATTENDED THERAPY | Y/N | | | | | | | |
| TROUBLE SLEEPING | 0-5 | | | | | | | |
| SELF-CARE ACTIVITIES | Y/N | | | | | | | |
| LOGGED DIARY | Y/N | | | | | | | |
| VISUALS: OBJECTS FURTHER AWAY OR CLOSER | 0-5 | | | | | | | |
| VISUALS: VIVID COLOURS OR BRIGHTNESS | Y/N | | | | | | | |
| AUDIO PERCEPTION PROBLEMS E.G. ALTERED VOICE | 0-5 | | | | | | | |
| ENGAGED IN SOCIAL ACTIVITIES | Y/N | | | | | | | |
| SELF ESTEEM | 0-5 | | | | | | | |
| USED COPING SKILLS | Y/N | | | | | | | |

USE THIS CHART TO TRACK DAILY MOODS, SYMPTOMS AND HABITS. KEEP AN EYE IF THINGS CHANGE AND HOW YOU FEEL AFTER MAKING POSITIVE STEPS.

# DEREALIZATION DEPERSONALIZATION DISORDER MENTAL HEALTH AND SYMPTOM CHECK LIST
## PUT TIME STAMP, Y/N OR 0-5 FOR SEVERITY

| | FREQ. / SEVERITY Y/N | MON | TUES | WED | THURS | FRI | SAT | SUN |
|---|---|---|---|---|---|---|---|---|
| RELATIONSHIP PROBLEMS | Y/N | | | | | | | |
| OVERSLEEPING | 0-5 | | | | | | | |
| FEELING ON AUTOPILOT OR ROBOT | 0-5 | | | | | | | |
| GOING BLANK | 0-5 | | | | | | | |
| PANIC ATTACKS | Y/N | | | | | | | |
| FEELING FEARFUL | Y/N | | | | | | | |
| FEELING AS IF YOU ARE NOT REAL | Y/N | | | | | | | |
| FEELING TIME SLOWED DOWN OR SPED UP | Y/N | | | | | | | |
| FEELING PARALYSIS UNABLE TO MOVE | Y/N | | | | | | | |
| PEOPLE SEEM UNFAMILIAR | Y/N | | | | | | | |
| ENVIRONMENTS SEEM UNFAMILIAR | 0-5 | | | | | | | |
| OBSERVING INTERNAL SENSATIONS | Y/N | | | | | | | |
| FEELING FOGGY | Y/N | | | | | | | |
| OVERTHINKING | 0-5 | | | | | | | |
| CONFUSION | Y/N | | | | | | | |
| DISORGANISATION | 0-5 | | | | | | | |
| DIFFICULTY CONCENTRATING | Y/N | | | | | | | |
| DIFFICULTY COMPLETING TASKS | Y/N | | | | | | | |
| FEELING IRRITABLE | 0-5 | | | | | | | |
| EXPERIENCED RELATIONSHIP PROBLEMS | Y/N | | | | | | | |
| FEELING DETACHED | 0-5 | | | | | | | |
| DECREASED SENSATIONS | Y/N | | | | | | | |
| CONSUMED ALCOHOL | 0-5 | | | | | | | |
| CONSUMED RECREATIONAL DRUGS | Y/N | | | | | | | |

USE THIS CHART TO TRACK DAILY MOODS, SYMPTOMS AND HABITS. KEEP AN EYE IF THINGS CHANGE AND HOW YOU FEEL AFTER MAKING POSITIVE STEPS.

| | FREQ. / SEVERITY Y/N | MON | TUES | WED | THURS | FRI | SAT | SUN |
|---|---|---|---|---|---|---|---|---|
| EXERCISE | MINS | | | | | | | |
| FEELING CALM | 0-5 | | | | | | | |
| FEELING HAPPY | 0-5 | | | | | | | |
| FEELING PRODUCTIVE | 0-5 | | | | | | | |
| WORK/SCHOOL STRESS | 0-5 | | | | | | | |
| GENERAL STRESS | 0-5 | | | | | | | |
| SPOKE TO SOMEONE ABOUT FEELINGS | Y/N | | | | | | | |
| MEDICATION | DOSE | | | | | | | |
| MEDICATION | DOSE | | | | | | | |
| MEDICATION | DOSE | | | | | | | |
| MEDICATION | DOSE | | | | | | | |
| MEDICATION | DOSE | | | | | | | |

FILL IN THE CHARTS TO TRACK EVENTS, MOODS, TRIGGERS, THINGS YOU WANT TO CHANGE, DETAILED NOTES

_____
_____
_____
_____
_____
_____
_____
_____
_____
_____
_____
_____
_____
_____

HOW OFTEN WAS THIS CHART FILLED OUT?
NOT AT ALL   [ ]        1-3X PER WEEK   [ ]        ALMOST EVERY DAY   [ ]        EVERYDAY   [ ]

# TIME OF DAY SYMPTOM TRACKER

TRACK THE SEVERITY OF YOUR SYMPTOMS THROUGHOUT THE DAY USING THE
SCALE, USE THE NOTE SECTION BELOW TO LIST THE SYMPTOMS YOU EXPERIENCED.
USE THIS TO SEE IF CERTAIN TIMES OF DAY E.G. MEAL TIMES OR FIRST THING IN THE
MORNING, ARE TRIGGERS FOR YOU.

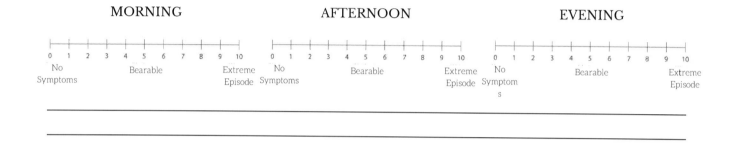

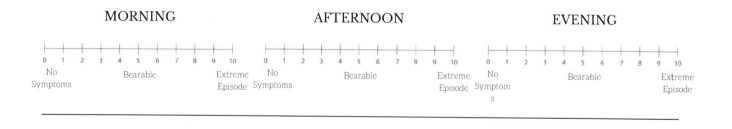

# GROUNDING TECHNIQUES

**WHAT CAN YOU SEE AROUND YOU? WHO OR WHAT SEEMS FAMILIAR? OR DESCRIBE A CALMING PLACE AND WHAT IT LOOKS LIKE.**

_____

_____

_____

_____

**TRY LISTENING TO THE SOUNDS AROUND YOU OR GO SOMEWHERE WITH FAMILIAR CALMING SOUNDS E.G. SOUNDS OF NATURE OR A FAVOURITE SONG. DESCRIBE THOSE SOUNDS.**

_____

_____

_____

_____

**USING ALL YOUR SENSES LIKE SMELL, TASTE, TOUCH, HEARING, DESCRIBE YOUR SURROUNDINGS OR YOUR FAVOURITE EXPERIENCES E.G. FAVOURITE FOOD.**

_____

_____

_____

_____

**HOW DO YOU CURRENTLY FEEL? AND WHAT DO YOU THINK ABOUT HOW YOU CURRENTLY FEEL? CAN YOU CHALLENGE THOSE THOUGHTS?**

_____

_____

_____

_____

**WHAT IS YOUR PREFERRED GROUNDING TECHNIQUE? E.G. BREATHING SLOWLY? DISTRACTING YOURSELF? MAKE A LIST OF TECHNIQUES YOU CAN USE WHEN YOU FEEL YOUR SYMPTOMS ARE BAD OR YOUR ANXIETY OR MOOD AROUND THEM ARE TROUBLING YOU.**

_____

_____

_____

_____

# PRACTICAL STRATEGIES FOR DISOCCIATION

TRIGGER WARNING:
WHAT MAY HELP ONE PERSON MAY TRIGGER OTHERS, USE THESE TECHNIQUES WITH CAUTION AND MODIFY THEM AROUND YOU.

**WHAT SITUATIONS DO YOU FIND TRIGGERING OR EXACERBATE YOUR DEPERSONALIZATION/DEREALIZATION?**

_____

_____

_____

_____

**WHAT FEATURES DO THESE SCENARIOS SHARE? ARE THEY STRESSFUL? UPSETTING? RANDOM? INVOLVE FAMILY? PAST TRAUMA?**

_____

_____

_____

_____

**HOW DO YOU FEEL DURING THESE EVENTS? WHAT ARE YOU SYMPTOMS AND EMOTIONS, AND WHAT ARE YOUR THOUGHTS ON THEM?**

_____

_____

_____

_____

**HOW CAN YOU PREPARE FOR THESE SITUATIONS IN THE FUTURE?**

_____

_____

_____

_____

**WHAT CHANGES CAN I MAKE TO IMPROVE MY SYMPTOMS AND FEELINGS DURING (OR AFTER) THESE SYMPTOMS? (E.G. GROUNDING TECHNIQUES, CHANGING THOUGHT PATTERNS, CALMING RITUALS TO LOWER STRESS LEVELS DURING SOCIAL SITUATIONS ETC)**

_____

_____

_____

_____

# TIME OF DAY ANXIETY & MOOD TRACKER

TRACK YOUR ANXIETY FLUCTUATIONS THROUGHOUT THE DAY TO SPOT POSSIBLE
TRIGGERS AND PATTERNS TO MANAGE YOUR STRESS/ANXIETY LEVELS MORE
EFFECTIVELY. WRITE TRIGGERS AND COPING MECHANISMS IN THE NOTES.

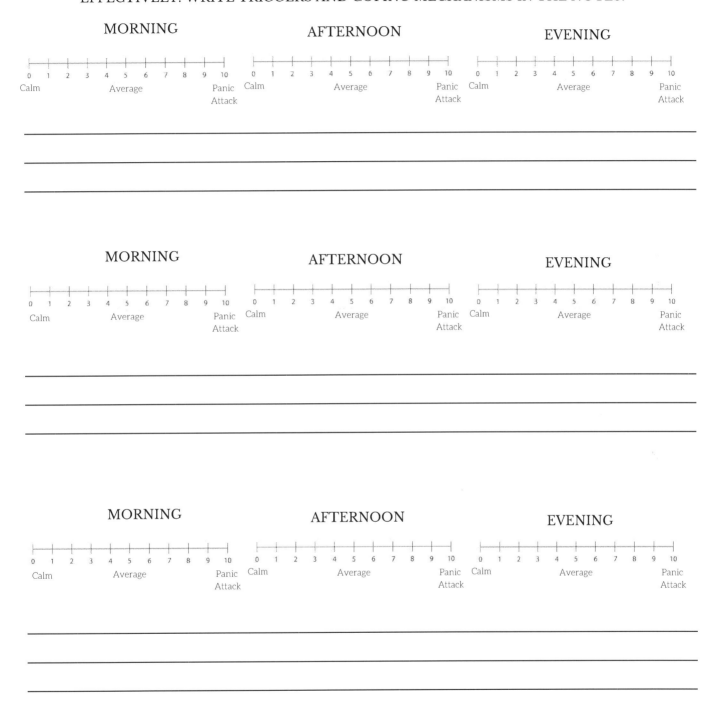

# GENERALIZED ANXIETY OVERVIEW WORKSHEET

WHAT SITUATIONS MAKE ME FEEL ANXIOUS?

_____
_____
_____
_____
_____

WHAT THOUGHTS DO I HAVE DURING EPISODES OF ANXIETY?
(TAKE A NOTE OF NEGATIVE THOUGHTS ABOUT YOURSELF AND YOUR ABILITY TO HANDLE THE SITUATION)

_____
_____
_____
_____

IS THERE ANYTHING FLAWED IN MY THINKING DURING THESE EPISODES?

_____
_____
_____
_____

WHAT IS THE REALITY OF THE SITUATION AND WHAT CAN I THINK INSTEAD?

_____
_____
_____
_____

WHAT CHANGES CAN I MAKE TO IMPROVE MY ANXIETY DURING THIS SITUATION?
(E.G. CHANGING THOUGHT PATTERNS, CALMING RITUALS TO LOWER STRESS LEVELS
DURING SITUATIONS ETC)

_____
_____
_____
_____

# SLEEP TRACKER

| TOTAL SLEEP TIME | SLEEP START TIME | WAKE UP TIME | NAP TIMES | DATE |
|---|---|---|---|---|
| | | | | |
| | | | | |
| | | | | |
| | | | | |
| | | | | |
| | | | | |
| | | | | |
| | | | | |
| | | | | |
| | | | | |
| | | | | |
| | | | | |

# SYMPTOM TRACKER

| DATE | TIME | DURATION | DESCRIPTION |
|------|------|----------|-------------|
|      |      |          |             |
|      |      |          |             |
|      |      |          |             |
|      |      |          |             |
|      |      |          |             |
|      |      |          |             |
|      |      |          |             |
|      |      |          |             |
|      |      |          |             |
|      |      |          |             |
|      |      |          |             |
|      |      |          |             |
|      |      |          |             |
|      |      |          |             |
|      |      |          |             |
|      |      |          |             |
|      |      |          |             |
|      |      |          |             |
|      |      |          |             |
|      |      |          |             |
|      |      |          |             |
|      |      |          |             |
|      |      |          |             |
|      |      |          |             |
|      |      |          |             |
|      |      |          |             |
|      |      |          |             |
|      |      |          |             |
|      |      |          |             |
|      |      |          |             |
|      |      |          |             |

Self Care
is not
Selfish.
It's self respect.

# DAILY ENERGY vs MOOD TRACKER

TRACK YOUR DAILY ENERGY AND MOOD USING DIFFERENT COLOURS ON THIS LINE CHART - NOTE YOUR TRIGGERS BELOW.

100

75

50

25

0

ENERGY

| MONDAY | TUESDAY | WEDNESDAY | THURSDAY | FRIDAY | SATURDAY | SUNDAY |

MOOD

# DEREALIZATION DEPERSONALIZATION DISORDER MENTAL HEALTH AND SYMPTOM CHECK LIST
PUT TIME STAMP, Y/N OR 0-5 FOR SEVERITY

| | FREQ. / SEVERITY Y/N | MON | TUES | WED | THURS | FRI | SAT | SUN |
|---|---|---|---|---|---|---|---|---|
| OVERALL MOOD | 0-5 | | | | | | | |
| ENERGY LEVELS | 0-5 | | | | | | | |
| ANXIETY | 0-5 | | | | | | | |
| AMNESIA / MEMORY PROBLEMS | 0-5 | | | | | | | |
| FEELING DETACHED FROM THOUGHTS | Y/N | | | | | | | |
| FEELING DETACHED/ OUTSIDE FROM BODY | Y/N | | | | | | | |
| THINGS FEELING "UNREAL" OR "DREAM LIKE" | Y/N | | | | | | | |
| DEPRESSION | Y/N | | | | | | | |
| EMOTIONAL NUMBNESS | Y/N | | | | | | | |
| RAPID CYCLING MOOD SWINGS | Y/N | | | | | | | |
| FEELING OVERWHELMED | 0-5 | | | | | | | |
| EXPERIENCED FLASHBACKS | Y/N | | | | | | | |
| SENSORY CHANGES E.G. TASTE, SMELL | Y/N | | | | | | | |
| LACK OF MOTIVATION | 0-5 | | | | | | | |
| ATTENDED THERAPY | Y/N | | | | | | | |
| TROUBLE SLEEPING | 0-5 | | | | | | | |
| SELF-CARE ACTIVITIES | Y/N | | | | | | | |
| LOGGED DIARY | Y/N | | | | | | | |
| VISUALS: OBJECTS FURTHER AWAY OR CLOSER | 0-5 | | | | | | | |
| VISUALS: VIVID COLOURS OR BRIGHTNESS | Y/N | | | | | | | |
| AUDIO PERCEPTION PROBLEMS E.G. ALTERED VOICE | 0-5 | | | | | | | |
| ENGAGED IN SOCIAL ACTIVITIES | Y/N | | | | | | | |
| SELF ESTEEM | 0-5 | | | | | | | |
| USED COPING SKILLS | Y/N | | | | | | | |

USE THIS CHART TO TRACK DAILY MOODS, SYMPTOMS AND HABITS. KEEP AN EYE IF THINGS CHANGE AND HOW YOU FEEL AFTER MAKING POSITIVE STEPS.

# DEREALIZATION DEPERSONALIZATION DISORDER MENTAL HEALTH AND SYMPTOM CHECK LIST
## PUT TIME STAMP, Y/N OR 0-5 FOR SEVERITY

| | FREQ. / SEVERITY Y/N | MON | TUES | WED | THURS | FRI | SAT | SUN |
|---|---|---|---|---|---|---|---|---|
| RELATIONSHIP PROBLEMS | Y/N | | | | | | | |
| OVERSLEEPING | 0-5 | | | | | | | |
| FEELING ON AUTOPILOT OR ROBOT | 0-5 | | | | | | | |
| GOING BLANK | 0-5 | | | | | | | |
| PANIC ATTACKS | Y/N | | | | | | | |
| FEELING FEARFUL | Y/N | | | | | | | |
| FEELING AS IF YOU ARE NOT REAL | Y/N | | | | | | | |
| FEELING TIME SLOWED DOWN OR SPED UP | Y/N | | | | | | | |
| FEELING PARALYSIS UNABLE TO MOVE | Y/N | | | | | | | |
| PEOPLE SEEM UNFAMILIAR | Y/N | | | | | | | |
| ENVIRONMENTS SEEM UNFAMILIAR | 0-5 | | | | | | | |
| OBSERVING INTERNAL SENSATIONS | Y/N | | | | | | | |
| FEELING FOGGY | Y/N | | | | | | | |
| OVERTHINKING | 0-5 | | | | | | | |
| CONFUSION | Y/N | | | | | | | |
| DISORGANISATION | 0-5 | | | | | | | |
| DIFFICULTY CONCENTRATING | Y/N | | | | | | | |
| DIFFICULTY COMPLETING TASKS | Y/N | | | | | | | |
| FEELING IRRITABLE | 0-5 | | | | | | | |
| EXPERIENCED RELATIONSHIP PROBLEMS | Y/N | | | | | | | |
| FEELING DETACHED | 0-5 | | | | | | | |
| DECREASED SENSATIONS | Y/N | | | | | | | |
| CONSUMED ALCOHOL | 0-5 | | | | | | | |
| CONSUMED RECREATIONAL DRUGS | Y/N | | | | | | | |

USE THIS CHART TO TRACK DAILY MOODS, SYMPTOMS AND HABITS. KEEP AN EYE IF THINGS CHANGE AND HOW YOU FEEL AFTER MAKING POSITIVE STEPS.

| | FREQ. / SEVERITY Y/N | MON | TUES | WED | THURS | FRI | SAT | SUN |
|---|---|---|---|---|---|---|---|---|
| EXERCISE | MINS | | | | | | | |
| FEELING CALM | 0-5 | | | | | | | |
| FEELING HAPPY | 0-5 | | | | | | | |
| FEELING PRODUCTIVE | 0-5 | | | | | | | |
| WORK/SCHOOL STRESS | 0-5 | | | | | | | |
| GENERAL STRESS | 0-5 | | | | | | | |
| SPOKE TO SOMEONE ABOUT FEELINGS | Y/N | | | | | | | |
| MEDICATION | DOSE | | | | | | | |
| MEDICATION | DOSE | | | | | | | |
| MEDICATION | DOSE | | | | | | | |
| MEDICATION | DOSE | | | | | | | |
| MEDICATION | DOSE | | | | | | | |

FILL IN THE CHARTS TO TRACK EVENTS, MOODS, TRIGGERS, THINGS YOU WANT TO CHANGE, DETAILED NOTES

_____
_____
_____
_____
_____
_____
_____
_____
_____
_____
_____
_____
_____
_____

HOW OFTEN WAS THIS CHART FILLED OUT?
NOT AT ALL    [ ]        1-3X PER WEEK   [ ]        ALMOST EVERY DAY   [ ]        EVERYDAY  [ ]

# TIME OF DAY SYMPTOM TRACKER

TRACK THE SEVERITY OF YOUR SYMPTOMS THROUGHOUT THE DAY USING THE SCALE, USE THE NOTE SECTION BELOW TO LIST THE SYMPTOMS YOU EXPERIENCED. USE THIS TO SEE IF CERTAIN TIMES OF DAY E.G. MEAL TIMES OR FIRST THING IN THE MORNING, ARE TRIGGERS FOR YOU.

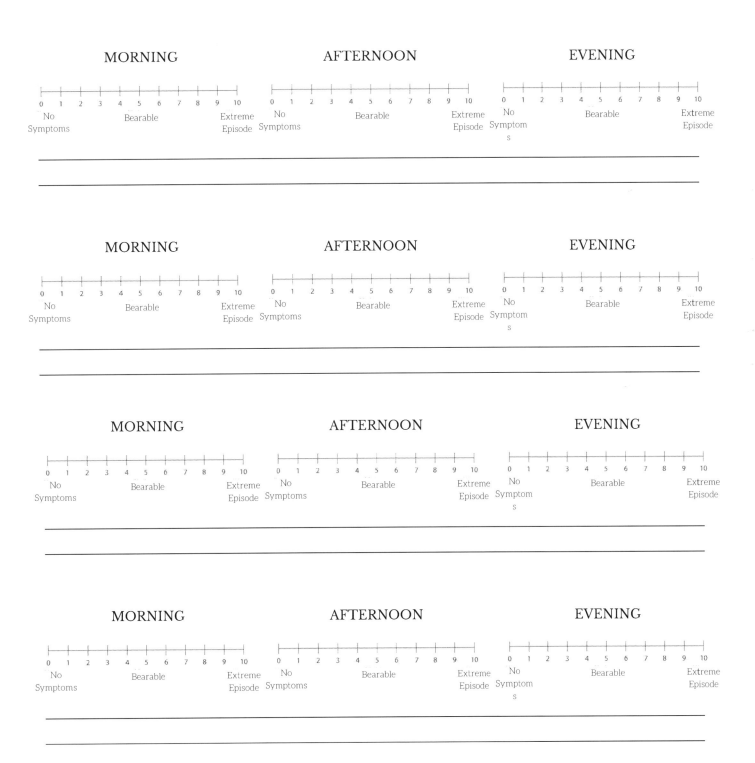

### MORNING

0 1 2 3 4 5 6 7 8 9 10

No Symptoms    Bearable    Extreme Episode

### AFTERNOON

0 1 2 3 4 5 6 7 8 9 10

No Symptoms    Bearable    Extreme Episode

### EVENING

0 1 2 3 4 5 6 7 8 9 10

No Symptoms    Bearable    Extreme Episode

---

### MORNING

0 1 2 3 4 5 6 7 8 9 10

No Symptoms    Bearable    Extreme Episode

### AFTERNOON

0 1 2 3 4 5 6 7 8 9 10

No Symptoms    Bearable    Extreme Episode

### EVENING

0 1 2 3 4 5 6 7 8 9 10

No Symptoms    Bearable    Extreme Episode

---

### MORNING

0 1 2 3 4 5 6 7 8 9 10

No Symptoms    Bearable    Extreme Episode

### AFTERNOON

0 1 2 3 4 5 6 7 8 9 10

No Symptoms    Bearable    Extreme Episode

### EVENING

0 1 2 3 4 5 6 7 8 9 10

No Symptoms    Bearable    Extreme Episode

---

### MORNING

0 1 2 3 4 5 6 7 8 9 10

No Symptoms    Bearable    Extreme Episode

### AFTERNOON

0 1 2 3 4 5 6 7 8 9 10

No Symptoms    Bearable    Extreme Episode

### EVENING

0 1 2 3 4 5 6 7 8 9 10

No Symptoms    Bearable    Extreme Episode

# GROUNDING TECHNIQUES

**WHAT CAN YOU SEE AROUND YOU? WHO OR WHAT SEEMS FAMILIAR? OR DESCRIBE A CALMING PLACE AND WHAT IT LOOKS LIKE.**

**TRY LISTENING TO THE SOUNDS AROUND YOU OR GO SOMEWHERE WITH FAMILIAR CALMING SOUNDS E.G. SOUNDS OF NATURE OR A FAVOURITE SONG. DESCRIBE THOSE SOUNDS.**

**USING ALL YOUR SENSES LIKE SMELL, TASTE, TOUCH, HEARING, DESCRIBE YOUR SURROUNDINGS OR YOUR FAVOURITE EXPERIENCES E.G. FAVOURITE FOOD.**

**HOW DO YOU CURRENTLY FEEL? AND WHAT DO YOU THINK ABOUT HOW YOU CURRENTLY FEEL? CAN YOU CHALLENGE THOSE THOUGHTS?**

**WHAT IS YOUR PREFERRED GROUNDING TECHNIQUE? E.G. BREATHING SLOWLY? DISTRACTING YOURSELF? MAKE A LIST OF TECHNIQUES YOU CAN USE WHEN YOU FEEL YOUR SYMPTOMS ARE BAD OR YOUR ANXIETY OR MOOD AROUND THEM ARE TROUBLING YOU.**

# PRACTICAL STRATEGIES FOR DISOCCIATION

TRIGGER WARNING:
WHAT MAY HELP ONE PERSON MAY TRIGGER OTHERS, USE THESE TECHNIQUES WITH CAUTION AND MODIFY THEM AROUND YOU.

## WHAT SITUATIONS DO YOU FIND TRIGGERING OR EXACERBATE YOUR DEPERSONALIZATION/DEREALIZATION?

## WHAT FEATURES DO THESE SCENARIOS SHARE? ARE THEY STRESSFUL? UPSETTING? RANDOM? INVOLVE FAMILY? PAST TRAUMA?

## HOW DO YOU FEEL DURING THESE EVENTS? WHAT ARE YOU SYMPTOMS AND EMOTIONS, AND WHAT ARE YOUR THOUGHTS ON THEM?

## HOW CAN YOU PREPARE FOR THESE SITUATIONS IN THE FUTURE?

## WHAT CHANGES CAN I MAKE TO IMPROVE MY SYMPTOMS AND FEELINGS DURING (OR AFTER) THESE SYMPTOMS? (E.G. GROUNDING TECHNIQUES, CHANGING THOUGHT PATTERNS, CALMING RITUALS TO LOWER STRESS LEVELS DURING SOCIAL SITUATIONS ETC)

# TIME OF DAY ANXIETY & MOOD TRACKER

TRACK YOUR ANXIETY FLUCTUATIONS THROUGHOUT THE DAY TO SPOT POSSIBLE
TRIGGERS AND PATTERNS TO MANAGE YOUR STRESS/ANXIETY LEVELS MORE
EFFECTIVELY. WRITE TRIGGERS AND COPING MECHANISMS IN THE NOTES.

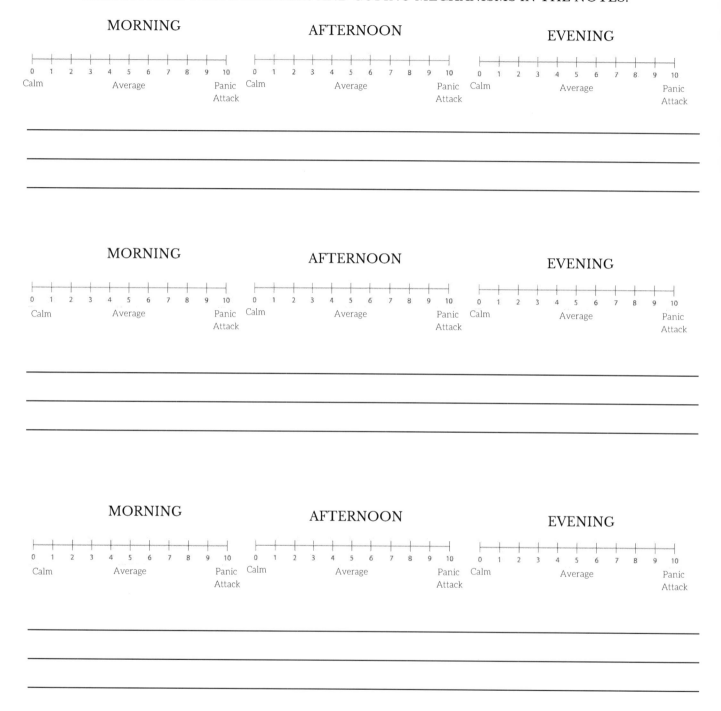

# GENERALIZED ANXIETY OVERVIEW WORKSHEET

WHAT SITUATIONS MAKE ME FEEL ANXIOUS?

_____
_____
_____
_____
_____

WHAT THOUGHTS DO I HAVE DURING EPISODES OF ANXIETY?
(TAKE A NOTE OF NEGATIVE THOUGHTS ABOUT YOURSELF AND YOUR ABILITY TO HANDLE THE SITUATION)

_____
_____
_____
_____
_____

IS THERE ANYTHING FLAWED IN MY THINKING DURING THESE EPISODES?

_____
_____
_____
_____
_____

WHAT IS THE REALITY OF THE SITUATION AND WHAT CAN I THINK INSTEAD?

_____
_____
_____
_____

WHAT CHANGES CAN I MAKE TO IMPROVE MY ANXIETY DURING THIS SITUATION?
(E.G. CHANGING THOUGHT PATTERNS, CALMING RITUALS TO LOWER STRESS LEVELS
DURING SITUATIONS ETC)

_____
_____
_____
_____

# SLEEP TRACKER

| TOTAL SLEEP TIME | SLEEP START TIME | WAKE UP TIME | NAP TIMES | DATE |
|---|---|---|---|---|
|  |  |  |  |  |
|  |  |  |  |  |
|  |  |  |  |  |
|  |  |  |  |  |
|  |  |  |  |  |
|  |  |  |  |  |
|  |  |  |  |  |
|  |  |  |  |  |
|  |  |  |  |  |
|  |  |  |  |  |
|  |  |  |  |  |
|  |  |  |  |  |

# SYMPTOM TRACKER

| DATE | TIME | DURATION | DESCRIPTION |
|------|------|----------|-------------|
|      |      |          |             |
|      |      |          |             |
|      |      |          |             |
|      |      |          |             |
|      |      |          |             |
|      |      |          |             |
|      |      |          |             |
|      |      |          |             |
|      |      |          |             |
|      |      |          |             |
|      |      |          |             |
|      |      |          |             |
|      |      |          |             |
|      |      |          |             |
|      |      |          |             |
|      |      |          |             |
|      |      |          |             |
|      |      |          |             |
|      |      |          |             |
|      |      |          |             |
|      |      |          |             |
|      |      |          |             |
|      |      |          |             |
|      |      |          |             |
|      |      |          |             |
|      |      |          |             |
|      |      |          |             |
|      |      |          |             |
|      |      |          |             |
|      |      |          |             |
|      |      |          |             |

# *WHAT HAVE YOU DONE IN YOUR LIFE THAT HAS MADE SOMEONE ELSE HAPPY?*

ANSWER THESE QUESTIONS TO BREAK OUT OF NEGATIVE THOUGHT PATTERNS AND REFOCUS ON THE THINGS THAT MAKE YOU HAPPY AND GRATEFUL.

# DAILY ENERGY vs MOOD TRACKER

TRACK YOUR DAILY ENERGY AND MOOD USING DIFFERENT COLOURS ON THIS LINE CHART - NOTE YOUR TRIGGERS BELOW.

100

75

50

25

0

ENERGY | MONDAY | TUESDAY | WEDNESDAY | THURSDAY | FRIDAY | SATURDAY | SUNDAY | MOOD

# DEREALIZATION DEPERSONALIZATION DISORDER MENTAL HEALTH AND SYMPTOM CHECK LIST
PUT TIME STAMP, Y/N OR 0-5 FOR SEVERITY

| | FREQ. / SEVERITY Y/N | MON | TUES | WED | THURS | FRI | SAT | SUN |
|---|---|---|---|---|---|---|---|---|
| OVERALL MOOD | 0-5 | | | | | | | |
| ENERGY LEVELS | 0-5 | | | | | | | |
| ANXIETY | 0-5 | | | | | | | |
| AMNESIA / MEMORY PROBLEMS | 0-5 | | | | | | | |
| FEELING DETACHED FROM THOUGHTS | Y/N | | | | | | | |
| FEELING DETACHED/ OUTSIDE FROM BODY | Y/N | | | | | | | |
| THINGS FEELING "UNREAL" OR "DREAM LIKE" | Y/N | | | | | | | |
| DEPRESSION | Y/N | | | | | | | |
| EMOTIONAL NUMBNESS | Y/N | | | | | | | |
| RAPID CYCLING MOOD SWINGS | Y/N | | | | | | | |
| FEELING OVERWHELMED | 0-5 | | | | | | | |
| EXPERIENCED FLASHBACKS | Y/N | | | | | | | |
| SENSORY CHANGES E.G. TASTE, SMELL | Y/N | | | | | | | |
| LACK OF MOTIVATION | 0-5 | | | | | | | |
| ATTENDED THERAPY | Y/N | | | | | | | |
| TROUBLE SLEEPING | 0-5 | | | | | | | |
| SELF-CARE ACTIVITIES | Y/N | | | | | | | |
| LOGGED DIARY | Y/N | | | | | | | |
| VISUALS: OBJECTS FURTHER AWAY OR CLOSER | 0-5 | | | | | | | |
| VISUALS: VIVID COLOURS OR BRIGHTNESS | Y/N | | | | | | | |
| AUDIO PERCEPTION PROBLEMS E.G. ALTERED VOICE | 0-5 | | | | | | | |
| ENGAGED IN SOCIAL ACTIVITIES | Y/N | | | | | | | |
| SELF ESTEEM | 0-5 | | | | | | | |
| USED COPING SKILLS | Y/N | | | | | | | |

USE THIS CHART TO TRACK DAILY MOODS, SYMPTOMS AND HABITS. KEEP AN EYE IF THINGS CHANGE AND HOW YOU FEEL AFTER MAKING POSITIVE STEPS.

# DEREALIZATION DEPERSONALIZATION DISORDER MENTAL HEALTH AND SYMPTOM CHECK LIST
PUT TIME STAMP, Y/N OR 0-5 FOR SEVERITY

| | FREQ. / SEVERITY Y/N | MON | TUES | WED | THURS | FRI | SAT | SUN |
|---|---|---|---|---|---|---|---|---|
| RELATIONSHIP PROBLEMS | Y/N | | | | | | | |
| OVERSLEEPING | 0-5 | | | | | | | |
| FEELING ON AUTOPILOT OR ROBOT | 0-5 | | | | | | | |
| GOING BLANK | 0-5 | | | | | | | |
| PANIC ATTACKS | Y/N | | | | | | | |
| FEELING FEARFUL | Y/N | | | | | | | |
| FEELING AS IF YOU ARE NOT REAL | Y/N | | | | | | | |
| FEELING TIME SLOWED DOWN OR SPED UP | Y/N | | | | | | | |
| FEELING PARALYSIS UNABLE TO MOVE | Y/N | | | | | | | |
| PEOPLE SEEM UNFAMILIAR | Y/N | | | | | | | |
| ENVIRONMENTS SEEM UNFAMILIAR | 0-5 | | | | | | | |
| OBSERVING INTERNAL SENSATIONS | Y/N | | | | | | | |
| FEELING FOGGY | Y/N | | | | | | | |
| OVERTHINKING | 0-5 | | | | | | | |
| CONFUSION | Y/N | | | | | | | |
| DISORGANISATION | 0-5 | | | | | | | |
| DIFFICULTY CONCENTRATING | Y/N | | | | | | | |
| DIFFICULTY COMPLETING TASKS | Y/N | | | | | | | |
| FEELING IRRITABLE | 0-5 | | | | | | | |
| EXPERIENCED RELATIONSHIP PROBLEMS | Y/N | | | | | | | |
| FEELING DETACHED | 0-5 | | | | | | | |
| DECREASED SENSATIONS | Y/N | | | | | | | |
| CONSUMED ALCOHOL | 0-5 | | | | | | | |
| CONSUMED RECREATIONAL DRUGS | Y/N | | | | | | | |

USE THIS CHART TO TRACK DAILY MOODS, SYMPTOMS AND HABITS. KEEP AN EYE IF THINGS CHANGE AND HOW YOU FEEL AFTER MAKING POSITIVE STEPS.

| | FREQ. / SEVERITY Y/N | MON | TUES | WED | THURS | FRI | SAT | SUN |
|---|---|---|---|---|---|---|---|---|
| EXERCISE | MINS | | | | | | | |
| FEELING CALM | 0-5 | | | | | | | |
| FEELING HAPPY | 0-5 | | | | | | | |
| FEELING PRODUCTIVE | 0-5 | | | | | | | |
| WORK/SCHOOL STRESS | 0-5 | | | | | | | |
| GENERAL STRESS | 0-5 | | | | | | | |
| SPOKE TO SOMEONE ABOUT FEELINGS | Y/N | | | | | | | |
| MEDICATION | DOSE | | | | | | | |
| MEDICATION | DOSE | | | | | | | |
| MEDICATION | DOSE | | | | | | | |
| MEDICATION | DOSE | | | | | | | |
| MEDICATION | DOSE | | | | | | | |

FILL IN THE CHARTS TO TRACK EVENTS, MOODS, TRIGGERS, THINGS YOU WANT TO CHANGE, DETAILED NOTES

_____
_____
_____
_____
_____
_____
_____
_____
_____
_____
_____
_____
_____
_____

HOW OFTEN WAS THIS CHART FILLED OUT?
NOT AT ALL   [ ]        1-3X PER WEEK   [ ]        ALMOST EVERY DAY   [ ]        EVERYDAY  [ ]

# TIME OF DAY SYMPTOM TRACKER

TRACK THE SEVERITY OF YOUR SYMPTOMS THROUGHOUT THE DAY USING THE SCALE, USE THE NOTE SECTION BELOW TO LIST THE SYMPTOMS YOU EXPERIENCED. USE THIS TO SEE IF CERTAIN TIMES OF DAY E.G. MEAL TIMES OR FIRST THING IN THE MORNING, ARE TRIGGERS FOR YOU.

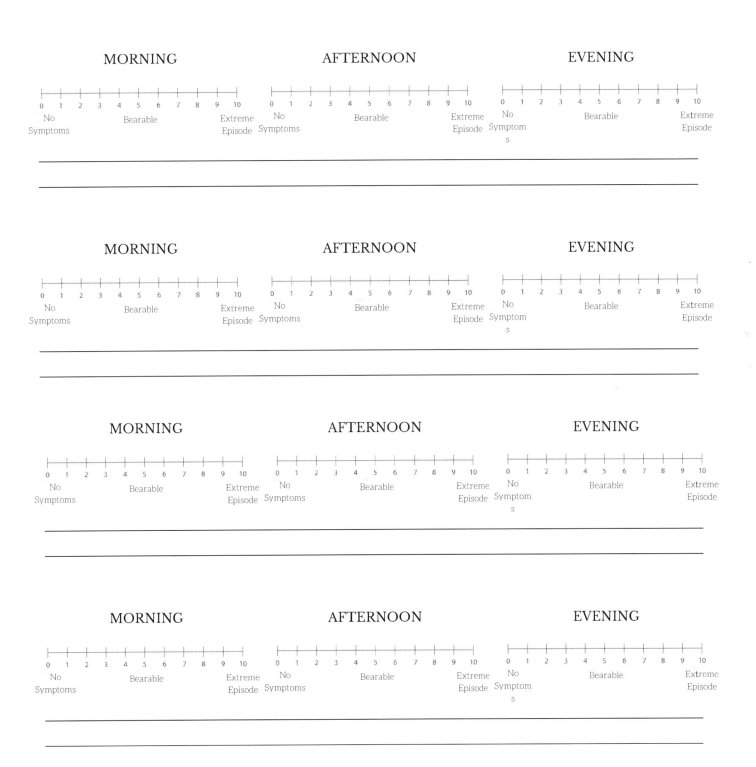

# GROUNDING TECHNIQUES

**WHAT CAN YOU SEE AROUND YOU? WHO OR WHAT SEEMS FAMILIAR? OR DESCRIBE A CALMING PLACE AND WHAT IT LOOKS LIKE.**

_____

_____

_____

_____

**TRY LISTENING TO THE SOUNDS AROUND YOU OR GO SOMEWHERE WITH FAMILIAR CALMING SOUNDS E.G. SOUNDS OF NATURE OR A FAVOURITE SONG. DESCRIBE THOSE SOUNDS.**

_____

_____

_____

_____

**USING ALL YOUR SENSES LIKE SMELL, TASTE, TOUCH, HEARING, DESCRIBE YOUR SURROUNDINGS OR YOUR FAVOURITE EXPERIENCES E.G. FAVOURITE FOOD.**

_____

_____

_____

_____

**HOW DO YOU CURRENTLY FEEL? AND WHAT DO YOU THINK ABOUT HOW YOU CURRENTLY FEEL? CAN YOU CHALLENGE THOSE THOUGHTS?**

_____

_____

_____

**WHAT IS YOUR PREFERRED GROUNDING TECHNIQUE? E.G. BREATHING SLOWLY? DISTRACTING YOURSELF? MAKE A LIST OF TECHNIQUES YOU CAN USE WHEN YOU FEEL YOUR SYMPTOMS ARE BAD OR YOUR ANXIETY OR MOOD AROUND THEM ARE TROUBLING YOU.**

_____

_____

_____

_____

# PRACTICAL STRATEGIES FOR DISOCCIATION

TRIGGER WARNING:
WHAT MAY HELP ONE PERSON MAY TRIGGER OTHERS, USE THESE TECHNIQUES WITH CAUTION AND MODIFY THEM AROUND YOU.

## WHAT SITUATIONS DO YOU FIND TRIGGERING OR EXACERBATE YOUR DEPERSONALIZATION/DEREALIZATION?

_____
_____
_____
_____
_____

## WHAT FEATURES DO THESE SCENARIOS SHARE? ARE THEY STRESSFUL? UPSETTING? RANDOM? INVOLVE FAMILY? PAST TRAUMA?

_____
_____
_____
_____

## HOW DO YOU FEEL DURING THESE EVENTS? WHAT ARE YOU SYMPTOMS AND EMOTIONS, AND WHAT ARE YOUR THOUGHTS ON THEM?

_____
_____
_____
_____
_____

## HOW CAN YOU PREPARE FOR THESE SITUATIONS IN THE FUTURE?

_____
_____
_____
_____

## WHAT CHANGES CAN I MAKE TO IMPROVE MY SYMPTOMS AND FEELINGS DURING (OR AFTER) THESE SYMPTOMS? (E.G. GROUNDING TECHNIQUES, CHANGING THOUGHT PATTERNS, CALMING RITUALS TO LOWER STRESS LEVELS DURING SOCIAL SITUATIONS ETC)

_____
_____
_____
_____

# TIME OF DAY ANXIETY & MOOD TRACKER

TRACK YOUR ANXIETY FLUCTUATIONS THROUGHOUT THE DAY TO SPOT POSSIBLE TRIGGERS AND PATTERNS TO MANAGE YOUR STRESS/ANXIETY LEVELS MORE EFFECTIVELY. WRITE TRIGGERS AND COPING MECHANISMS IN THE NOTES.

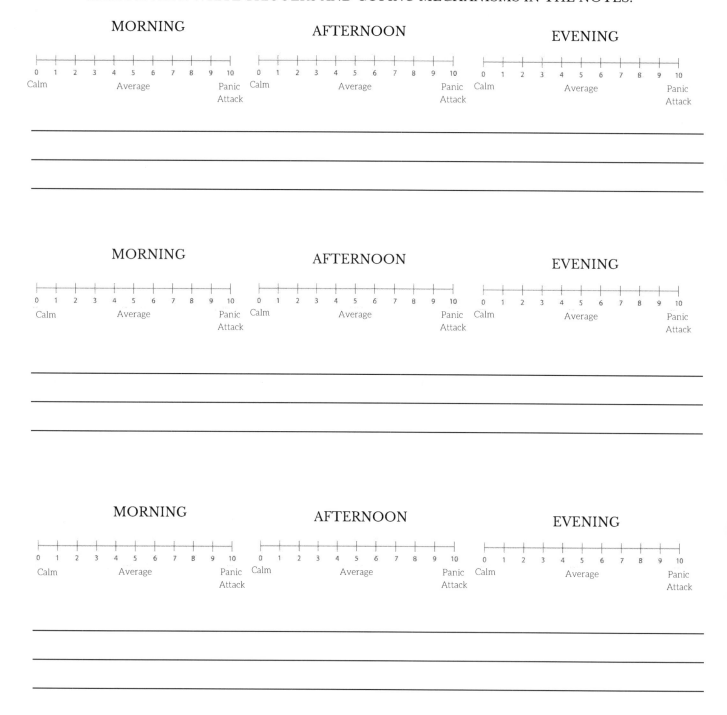

# GENERALIZED ANXIETY OVERVIEW WORKSHEET

WHAT SITUATIONS MAKE ME FEEL ANXIOUS?

_____
_____
_____
_____

WHAT THOUGHTS DO I HAVE DURING EPISODES OF ANXIETY?
(TAKE A NOTE OF NEGATIVE THOUGHTS ABOUT YOURSELF AND YOUR ABILITY TO HANDLE THE SITUATION)

_____
_____
_____
_____

IS THERE ANYTHING FLAWED IN MY THINKING DURING THESE EPISODES?

_____
_____
_____
_____

WHAT IS THE REALITY OF THE SITUATION AND WHAT CAN I THINK INSTEAD?

_____
_____
_____
_____

WHAT CHANGES CAN I MAKE TO IMPROVE MY ANXIETY DURING THIS SITUATION?
(E.G. CHANGING THOUGHT PATTERNS, CALMING RITUALS TO LOWER STRESS LEVELS
DURING SITUATIONS ETC)

_____
_____
_____
_____

# SLEEP TRACKER

| TOTAL SLEEP TIME | SLEEP START TIME | WAKE UP TIME | NAP TIMES | DATE |
|---|---|---|---|---|
| | | | | |
| | | | | |
| | | | | |
| | | | | |
| | | | | |
| | | | | |
| | | | | |
| | | | | |
| | | | | |
| | | | | |
| | | | | |

# SYMPTOM TRACKER

| DATE | TIME | DURATION | DESCRIPTION |
|------|------|----------|-------------|
| | | | |
| | | | |
| | | | |
| | | | |
| | | | |
| | | | |
| | | | |
| | | | |
| | | | |
| | | | |
| | | | |
| | | | |
| | | | |
| | | | |
| | | | |
| | | | |
| | | | |
| | | | |
| | | | |
| | | | |
| | | | |
| | | | |
| | | | |
| | | | |
| | | | |
| | | | |
| | | | |
| | | | |
| | | | |
| | | | |
| | | | |

# One Minute Meditation

Breathe in through your nose.

Breathe out through your mouth.

Feel air in the depths of your lungs
as you breathe in again.

As you breathe out feel tension
release from your body.

Repeat 3x.

# SAFETY PLAN - SELF HARM ALTERNATIVES / COPING METHODS

USE THIS TO WRITE METHODS OF HARM REDUCTION AND ALTERNATIVES TO SELF HARM, WHEN YOU USED THEM AND EFFECTIVENESS.

| COPING METHOD IDEA | MINIMUM DURATION | HOW WELL IT WORKED | DATE |
|---|---|---|---|
|  |  |  |  |
|  |  |  |  |
|  |  |  |  |
|  |  |  |  |
|  |  |  |  |
|  |  |  |  |
|  |  |  |  |
|  |  |  |  |
|  |  |  |  |
|  |  |  |  |
|  |  |  |  |
|  |  |  |  |
|  |  |  |  |
|  |  |  |  |
|  |  |  |  |
|  |  |  |  |
|  |  |  |  |
|  |  |  |  |

# EMERGENCY CONTACTS

THERE IS NO SHAME IN REACHING OUT, IT IS BETTER TO REACH OUT THAN TO SELF-HARM. IF YOU FEEL LIKE A DANGER TO YOURSELF PLEASE CALL EMERGENCY SERVICES AND A TRUSTED PERSON.

WRITE ALL EMERGENCY AND CRISIS CONTACT DETAILS FOR WHEN YOU ARE IN CRISIS BELOW AND CALL THEM IN AN EMERGENCY.

_____

_____

_____

_____

HTTPS://WWW.SAMARITANS.ORG/

GO TO THIS WEBSITE TO FIND RESOURCES AND WRITE THE RELEVANT CONTACT DETAILS

Manufactured by Amazon.ca
Bolton, ON

20785179R00098